SCOTLAND

THE HIGHE AND MIGHTIE PRINCE, Iames THE SIXT, BY THE GRACE OF GOD KINGE OF SCOTLANDE. R.E. *fecit*.

JAMES VI.

SCOTLAND

FROM THE EARLIEST TIMES TO THE
PRESENT CENTURY

BY

JOHN MACKINTOSH

BOOKS FOR LIBRARIES PRESS
FREEPORT, NEW YORK

First Published 1890
Reprinted 1972

INTERNATIONAL STANDARD BOOK NUMBER:
0-8369-6800-X

LIBRARY OF CONGRESS CATALOG CARD NUMBER:
75-39198

PRINTED IN THE UNITED STATES OF AMERICA
BY
NEW WORLD BOOK MANUFACTURING CO., INC.
HALLANDALE, FLORIDA 33009

PREFACE.

THE Story of Scotland presents two classes of facts and incidents of varied and absorbing interest. First, the conflict of the chief tribes with each other ; the foundation of the Monarchy ; the gradual extension of the kingdom from its centre outward ; and the development of a distinct and intense nationality. Second, the struggles arising from the invasions and attacks of external enemies, which were commenced by the Romans, followed by the Danes and Norwegians ; and, finally, the long and unequal struggle with England. In all these conflicts for liberty and independence, the Scots made a heroic and memorable defence. Although often cruelly oppressed and driven to the greatest extremities of suffering and privation, at times almost conquered; still in the face of all obstacles and against fearful odds they continued to resist and ultimately triumphed.

The subsequent internal struggles were political and religious. Owing to a series of events and circumstances the Scotch nobles for two centuries and a half were able to control the Crown and the Executive solely in their own interest. The religious contests connected with the Reformation, the conflict of the reformed clergy with the Crown ; the Covenanting struggle with its many stirring incidents—the Persecution, the Revolution, and the Disruption—which all present many features of surpassing interest.

After the Union, and the Risings of 1715 and 1745, the progress and the development of the nation in almost every department of human activity have been marvellous. The limits of this volume only permitted a brief reference to some of the many important subjects of the latest period; but it is hoped that what has been presented will prove interesting.

J. M.

Aberdeen,
June, 1890.

CONTENTS.

III.

IV.

V.

I *

LIST OF ILLUSTRATIONS.

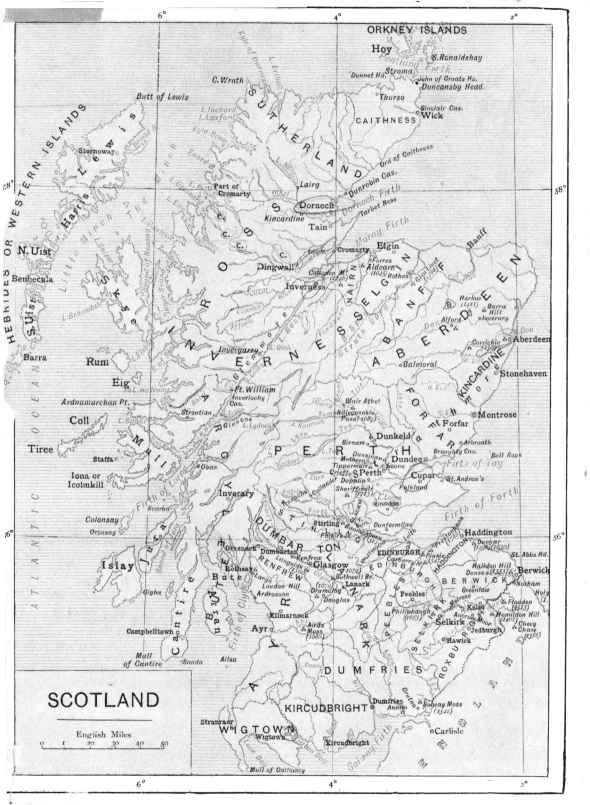

ORKNEY ISLANDS

SCOTLAND

English Miles
0   1   20   30   40   50

THE STORY OF SCOTLAND.

I.

EARLY HISTORY.

WHEN Man awoke from a long dream to conscious-
ness, and looked wistfully around him in amazement,
he readily snatched at anything, and believed in anything, that seemed to give him any explanation or
relieved his embarrassment. Thus the early histories
of most nations are enveloped in legends and myths ;
and Scotland has a legendary story touching the origin
of the early inhabitants of the country. One form of
our legend was that Gathelus, a Greek, with a band
of followers, went to Egypt about the time of the
Exodus, and, after performing many great actions,
was appointed commander-in-chief of the Egyptian
forces, and married Scota, Pharaoh's daughter. After
the destruction of the Egyptian army in the Red
Sea, he fled with his wife by way of the Medi-
terranean, landed in Portugal, and founded a kingdom in Brigantium, and there reigned as king. In
process of time a descendant of his became King of
Ireland, The Scots came from Ireland, and Fergus,

I

the son of Ferchand, was their first king on this side of the sea. So Fergus I. founded the Scottish monarchy, three centuries before the Christian era ; and a line of one hundred and ten kings succeeded and sat on the throne which he had established.

This story was put forward in support of the antiquity and independence of the kingdom, after the difficulties with England had arisen in the later years of the thirteenth century. In the disputes with England the long line of kings had some effect.

From evidence obtained by a different method it appears that Britain was inhabited in a far past age, at least several thousands of years before the Christian era. A people of the Basque race spread over the greater part of Europe before the arrival of any branch of the Aryan race, and were in possession of Britain at a remote period. But the traces of their occupation of the several parts of the island are scanty, consisting of stone objects and tools, and human remains, and they cannot be discussed in this volume, further than to say that, from the evidence, it seems probable that tribes akin to the Basques had penetrated into Scotland before the coming of the Celtic race.

The Celts were the first branch of the Aryan race who invaded Europe. They spread over a large part of it, and afterwards, at intervals, they were followed by other branches of the same race, and the newcomers pressed the Celts onward and outward. Thus began the long struggle which subsequently made European history.

It is highly probable that the Celtic race occupied

Scotland in the polished Stone Age, and gradually subdued and absorbed the race which had preceded them. There is evidence of various kinds to show that they had inhabited the country for a long period before the Roman invasion. They had domesticated animals and herds of cattle ; they had war-chariots and metallic weapons ; and they had attained to a certain degree of organisation and culture. Their religion was polytheistic. It consisted of a belief in supernatural beings, ghosts, and spirits, which pervaded nature, man, and animals, rivers, wells, and mountains. Very little indication of an organised heathen priesthood among the early Celtic tribes of Scotland has yet been found.

Julius Cæsar visited Britain forty-five years before the Christian era, but nearly a century elapsed ere the Romans made a determined effort to conquer the island. In the year A.D. 43, the real conquest of Britain was begun ; and by 77 the Roman province had been extended nearly to the Solway Firth. Agricola was appointed to the chief command in Britain in 78. In the summer of the following year, he appears to have advanced to the border counties of Scotland. In that region his advance was contested at every step by warlike tribes, who were unable, however, to withstand the disciplined Legions. Everywhere the inhabitants offered resistance ; and during the winter Agricola was engaged in bringing under subjection the territory overrun by his troops.

In 80 he determined to move northward and attack the Caledonians in their own strongholds. He penetrated nearly as far as the Firth of Tay, and secured, by erecting forts and outposts, some portions of the territories through which he had passed. His main line of defence he fixed on the ground lying between the Firths of Forth and Clyde, and the summer of 81 was spent in erecting a chain of forts along this line. Afterward he seems to have entered Fifeshire, and slowly advanced with the assistance of the Roman fleet toward the Tay. His army proceeded in three divisions not far apart from each other ; and the Caledonians resolved to attack one of them—the Ninth Legion. One night they assailed it, and fought their way through the gate and into the heart of the Roman camp ; but Agricola himself, with the fleetest of the horse and foot, came to the rescue. When day dawned the Caledonians had to fight the Ninth Legion on the one hand, and the reinforcement on the other, and the real struggle was at the gate of the camp. The Legions were victorious, and the Caledonians retired under cover of the marshes.

They were not disheartened. Agricola learned as the season passed that they were combining to strike a blow, and were removing their wives and children to places of safety. Both combatants were preparing for the struggle which was to determine whether the Romans were to obtain dominion over the whole island.

In the beginning of summer 86, Agricola sent his fleet round the coasts to ravage the seaboard and alarm the inhabitants. He then advanced with his army to Mons Grampius, and there the Caledonians were posted for battle. The native force numbered 30,000, under the command of Galgacus. As it was the custom for the leaders of armies to address their troops on the eve of a battle, so Tacitus the historian puts a speech into the mouth of Galgacus, the leader of the Caledonians, and a few sentences of it may be quoted :—

"When I reflect on the circumstances of our position, I feel a strong persuasion that our united efforts this day will prove the beginning of universal liberty to Britain. . . . In all the battles yet fought against the Romans, our countrymen may be deemed to have reposed their final hope in us ; for we, the noblest sons of Britain, and therefore stationed in its last recesses, far from the view of servile shores, have preserved even our eyes unpolluted by the contact of subjection. . . . Those plunderers of the world, after exhausting the land by their devastations, are rifling the ocean ; stimulated by avarice if their enemy be rich, by ambition if poor ; unsatiated by the East and by the West, the only people who behold wealth and indigence with equal avidity. To ravage, to slaughter, to usurp, under false titles, they call empire, and where they make a desert, they call it peace. . . . And shall not we, untouched, unsubdued, and struggling not for the acquisition, but for the security of liberty, show at the very first onset what men Caledonia has reserved for her defence ? Be not terrified by an idle show, and the glitter of silver and gold, which can neither protect nor wound. In the very ranks of the enemy we shall find our own bands. The Britons will acknowledge their own cause. The Gauls will recollect their former liberty. The rest of the Germans will desert them, as the

Usipii have lately done. Nor is there anything formidable behind them. Ungarrisoned towns, colonies of old men, municipal towns, distempered and distracted between unjust masters and ill-obeying subjects. There is a general ; here an army. There tributes, mines, and all the train of punishments inflicted on slaves, which, whether to bear eternally, or instantly to revenge, this field must determine. March, then, to battle, and think of your ancestors and of your posterity ! "

Agricola was afraid of being out-flanked, and extended his line to the utmost. His front consisted of 8,000 auxiliaries and 3,000 cavalry on the wings, the Legions or Roman soldiers were held in reserve ; and placed behind the centre. The Caledonian charioteers were moving on the ground between the two armies, and the footmen were posted on the heights. While the fighting was with missiles at a distance, the native troops held their ground, and their charioteers drove back the Roman cavalry ; but Agricola sent forward five cohorts to charge them with swords. For this weapon the natives were unprepared, and their first line fell back. The whole Roman line then advanced to the charge. Galgacus tried a flank movement with his reserve, but it failed ; the chariots became entangled in the broken ground, and a defeat ensued. They retreated, and attempted to check the pursuit of the Romans ; but many of the natives were slain. The Roman general did not pursue them beyond the Tay, but returned south to his winter quarters ; and shortly after he was recalled to Rome.

The Roman troops continued to have an incessant struggle with the northern tribes ; and forty years later the border counties were not within the lines of the empire. Between the years 120 and 138 the Romans built a wall from the river Tyne to the Solway Firth, which extended over seventy miles, and was strengthened at intervals by forts and towers. Soon afterwards they erected another wall, which commenced at Bridgeness on the Firth of Forth and

ROMAN URN.
(*Found at the Dean, Edinburgh.*)

crossed the country to near West Kilpatrick on the Clyde. This wall was the northern limit of the empire ; and it was the strip of territory on the south of it which the Romans occupied in Scotland, and even there they were never long permitted to hold undisputed possession.

By the middle of the fourth century the attacks of the Picts, the Scots, and other tribes upon the Roman

province had become extremely harassing. In 407
Constantine passed over to Gaul, withdrawing all
the available forces in Britain, and the Imperial sway
ceased in Scotland. The Roman occupation of a
portion of the country had failed to subdue the native
tribes, and it left no abiding impression.

When the Romans left the island, the tribes
occupying the part of the country which had been
subdued, formed the small kingdom of Strathclyde,
lying between the two Roman walls. After it was
cut off from the north of England by the encroachment of the Saxons, it comprised the counties of
Ayr, Lanark, Renfrew, and parts of Dumbarton,
Stirling, and Dumfries. The small state was exposed to the incessant attacks of the Saxons from
the south, and the Picts and Scots from the north
and the west. Although the Britons struggled hard
to defend their kingdom, it finally became absorbed
in the rest of Scotland early in the eleventh century.

The Picts were of the same race of tribes as those
whom the Romans called Caledonians. In the sixth
century they occupied the whole country on the north
of the Firths of Forth and Clyde, excepting the district
of Argyle which was held by the Scots. Southward
of the Forth, in Galloway the inhabitants were Picts,
that is, Celtic tribes. The Scots from Ireland seem
to have come and gone at different times ; but their
final settlement in Argyleshire and the neighbouring
isles was in the beginning of the sixth century. This
body of Scots consisted of the three sons of Erc—
Lorn, Fergus, and Angus—a tribe who sometimes
fought among themselves, and often came into

conflict with the Saxons and the Britons of Strathclyde. The Saxons entered the southern parts of
Scotland in the later half of the fifth century ; and
before the middle of the sixth they had established
themselves in Lothian. They pressed severely on the
Britons of Strathclyde, and extended their conquests
into the land of the Picts. In 685, Egfrid, their king,
attempted a bold stroke, crossed the Forth at Stirling,
and penetrated into the heart of the Pictish territory.
Continuing his advance he crossed the Tay, and in a
narrow pass of the Sidlaw Hills at Dunnichen, on the
20th of June, his army was attacked and utterly
defeated. The king was slain, and few of his army
escaped. This battle had the effect of severing the
district between the Tay and the Forth from the
influence which would have tended to make it a part
of England.

But the people south of the Forth in Lothian
remained essentially Saxon, and superseded the Celtic
inhabitants at an early period : there the Saxon speech
continued and gradually spread.

In the eighth century the Picts were the chief
power in Scotland. But their political organisation
resembled a rude confederacy more than a regularly constituted monarchy. In a word, the Picts
were a number of Celtic tribes, which sometimes on
great emergencies combined for the common defence
of the country. Besides the feuds incident to tribal
communities, the Picts, the Britons, the Scots, the
Saxons, and eventually the Danes or Norsemen,
carried on an intermissive warfare with one another.
In the seventh, eighth, and ninth centuries, these

tribes often met in conflict on a debateable territory between the Forth and the water of Almond, in the counties of Stirling and Linlithgow. The struggle between the tribes continued till a pretty complete nationality was formed.

The original centre of the historic kingdom was on the banks of the Tay at Scone, Perth, and Dunkeld. The venerated coronation stone was at Scone, and there the kings were installed to the throne. Perth was one of the chief towns of the country from the earliest period. Dunkeld, fourteen miles farther up the Tay, has always been the very gate to the Highlands ; and almost every invader of Caledonia has attempted to enter by this gorge and the route thence proceeding through the valleys of Athole, Badenoch, and Strathspey, to the northern Highlands. It must have been early observed that the plain of Strathmore, the Carse of Gowrie, and the Carse of Stirling, were worth fighting for ; and from the dawn of the historic period onward this becomes clearer.

In 839, the Danes invaded the territories of the Picts, and defeated them. Two years later Kenneth McAlpin obtained the small kingdom of the Scots in Argyle ; and in 844, he mounted the throne of the Picts at Scone. This was the natural result of the long struggle of the various tribes, as the accumulating force of circumstances and a common religion tended to a greater concentration of power under some one of the chief tribes. The actual kingdom which Kenneth McAlpin obtained only comprised a limited part of modern Scotland : it consisted of Argyle, the counties of Perth, Fife, and parts of Forfar, Dumbarton, and Stirling, with Scone, the Mount of Belief and Royalty, as its chief seat. The districts beyond this centre on the north-east, the north, the west, and south, were only gradually and with extreme difficulty subdued as the nation developed to its ultimate limits. After the establishment of the historic monarchy under McAlpin, the reigning monarchs were called kings of the Picts, then kings of Alban. Not till the tenth century was any part of the country called Scotland, but from the opening of the eleventh century this name gradually came to be applied to the whole country

II.

INTRODUCTION OF CHRISTIANITY

THE chief tribes, and the centre of the historic kingdom, having thus been indicated, some account must be given of the introduction of a new religion. Christianity was a prime factor in the development of Scotland. It became interwoven with the government, the institutions, the education, the literature, the music, the amusements, and the life of the people. Its influence operated from the cradle to the grave.

St. Ninian is amongst the earliest of the new teachers whose names have come down to us. He was the son of a British prince, and was educated in the Christian faith at Rome. His life was written by Ailred, a monk of the twelfth century, but it contains little reliable information. Bede lived nearer to the saint's time, and records that Ninian converted the southern Picts, and built a church of stone, which was unusual among them. This church was in Galloway at a spot called Whithern, and it developed into a monastery.

St. Ninian restored the sight of a king of Strathclyde, on whom God had inflicted the punishment of

blindness for his opposition, and when thus subdued
and healed, the king became a friend of the saint and
a ready supporter of the servants of Christ. He died
in 432, and was buried in his own church at Whithern.
His biographer affirmed that the relics of the saint
worked many miracles ; that at his tomb the sick
were cured, the lepers cleansed, the blind restored to
sight, and the wicked terrified. We know from later
sources that the relics of St. Ninian were objects of
veneration down to the Reformation. The best
evidence of the mission of St. Ninian in Scotland,
and his place in the grateful remembrance of the
people, is shown in the number of the churches
dedicated to his name. Churches were dedicated to
him in twenty-five counties stretching from Wigton to
Sutherland; upwards of sixty dedications to him have
been recorded.

In the middle of the sixth century St. Kentigern,
better known as St. Mungo, began his work amongst
the Britons of Strathclyde, where he encountered
many difficulties. The king and the people were all
heathens ; and in spite of St. Mungo's energy and
miracles, King Morken scorned his life and doctrine,
and publicly resisted him. When the saint asked for
some supplies of food to the monastery, the king
spurned his petition, and inflicted new injuries on him.
He said to the saint—" Cast thy care upon the Lord
and He will sustain thee, as thou hast often taught
others, that they who fear God shall lack nothing.
Thou though thou fearest God and keepeth His com-
mandments art in want of everything, even thy
necessary food ; while to me, who neither seek the

Kingdom of God nor the righteousness thereof, all prosperous things are added, and plenty of all sorts smileth upon me. Thy faith therefore is vain, and thy teaching false." The saint pleaded that it was part of the inscrutable ways of God to afflict just and holy men in this life, while the wicked were exalted by wealth. The king rose in a passion and said—"What more desirest thou? If trusting in thy God, without human hands, thou canst transfer to thy mansion all the corn in my barns, I yield with a glad mind and gift, and for the future will be devotedly obedient to thy requests."

When evening came the saint prayed earnestly. Then behold! the rain poured down in torrents, the waters of the Clyde rapidly rose into a flood and overflowed its banks where the king's barns were and carried them down the stream to the saint's dwelling, beside the Mollindinor burn which flows through Glasgow. But the miracle only enraged the king, who uttered many reproaches against the saint; and when he approached, the king rushed on him and struck him with his heel, and smote him to the ground upon his back. The time had come to manifest the Divine power on behalf of the injured saint. As Cathen, the king's adviser, had instigated the matter, so after mounting his horse to ride off, and laughing at the saint's discomfiture, his prancing steed stumbled and the rider fell backward, broke his neck, and expired. The king also was smitten with a swelling in his feet which ended in his death, and the same disease afflicted his family till it became extinct.

But the saint was forced to leave Strathclyde,

and went to Wales, where he laboured many years.
Afterward, when King Rederech reigned in Strathclyde, the saint returned and spent the remaining
years of his life amongst the Britons. He died about
the beginning of the seventh century. Under the
name of St. Mungo, he became the patron saint of
Glasgow, and was widely known and much revered in
Scotland. His tomb and relics at Glasgow were
objects of intense veneration down to the period of
the Reformation.

The most renowned of the saints who introduced
Christianity among the tribes of Scotland was St.
Columba. All have recognised in him the features of a
veritable hero. He was born of royal race at Gartan,
in the county of Donegal in Ireland, on the 7th of
December, 521. He was educated in his native land ;
and about the year 553, he founded the monastery
of Durrow, his chief institution in Ireland. It appears
that he was connected with some of the political
disputes of his countrymen ; but he left Ireland without any stigma on his character, and frequently re-
visited it, and everywhere met with the highest
respect.

In 563, Columba with twelve companions embarked
in a wicker boat covered with hides, and after touching
at Islay, landed and settled on the small isle of Iona.
It lay on the confines of the territories of the Scotch
and Pictish tribes : Connal, the king of the former,
gifted it to Columba ; and shortly after its possession
was confirmed to him by Brude, the king of the Picts.
There he founded his chief monastery, and thence
sent forth missionaries to convert the rude tribes of

the north of Scotland. The Scots of Argyle were then nominally Christians, but the Picts were not, and it was among the latter that Columba mostly laboured. He often visited the mainland, and gained an influence over its chiefs. In the year 565, Columba sought out the Pictish king's seat, which was on the south side of the river Ness, on or near the old Castle hill of Inverness. Brude in his pride had shut the gate against the holy man, but the saint, by the sign of the cross and knocking at it, caused it to fly open : Columba and his companions then entered, the king advanced and met them, and received the saint with due respect, and ever after honoured him.

Columba and his disciples preached the gospel among the Picts, baptized them, and founded many monasteries. Every monastery consisted of a body of clergy, who from these centres went out in circuits among the surrounding tribes to teach and convert them, and returned to their common home for shelter and support ; and in this way they gradually spread over the country.

A few incidents connected with Columba's action among the people may be narrated. When on a visit in the land of the Picts, he heard of a famous well which the heathen people worshipped. It had many evil qualities, and those who drank of it or washed in it were smitten with leprosy or some severe infirmity. Having learned the state of the case, he went boldly to the well, and then the Magi rejoiced, as they thought that he, too, would suffer from the touch of the baneful water ; but the saint raised his hands and invoked the name of Christ, then washed his hands, and with his disciples, drank of the water which he had blessed. Henceforth the demons departed from the well, and it never after injured any one, but, on the contrary, became famous for curing diseases.

In the account of St. Columba's life there is no evidence of an organised heathen priesthood in Scotland ; he was more engaged in fighting demons than Druidical priests. He went out one day to a sequestered spot in the woods to pray ; and when he began a host of black demons suddenly attacked him with iron darts : " But he, single-handed, against innumerable foes of such a nature, fought with the utmost bravery, having received the armour of the Apostle Paul. Thus the contest was maintained on both sides for the greater part of the day, nor could the demons, countless though they were, vanquish him, nor was he able by himself to drive them from the island, till the angels of God, as the saint afterward told certain persons, and they few in number, came to his aid, when the demons in terror gave way."

The sign of the cross was much employed. It was common to cross tools and implements before using them ; and in Columba's time there was an extensive use of charms which were produced by his blessing on a great variety of objects.

The form of Christianity introduced was essentially monastic. As Columba's institution of Iona was the centre of religious life in Scotland for two centuries, it presents the best example. The monastery of Iona consisted of a church with its altar and recesses, a refectory and kitchen, the huts of the monks, and the abbot's house, in which St. Columba read and wrote,

3

having several attendants awaiting his orders. All the buildings were inclosed by a wall, which was intended more for the restraint of the monks than for security. Outside the wall there were erections for cows, horses, grain, and agricultural implements ; for the monks heartily engaged in the labour of the field. The church and all the buildings were primitive structures formed of wood.

The Abbot was the head of the community, and his authority extended over all the monasteries and churches founded by Columba. Bishops in Iona and Scotland in the lifetime of Columba, and for two centuries after, were subject to the Abbots of Iona. St. Columba named his own successor, and afterwards a preference was given in the election of the Abbot to the founder's kin. Thus the sentiment of clanship entered strongly into the constitution of the Columbian monasteries.

The members of the monastery were summoned to the church by a bell, and at night they carried lanterns. The chief service was the solemn mass, when the offices were chanted and certain saints commemorated by name. On special occasions the Abbot summoned the monks by the toll of the bell to the church in the dead of night, addressed them, asked their prayers, then kneeled himself at the altar and prayed.

Besides the religious services, the stated employment of the Columbian community was reading, writing, and manual labour. The manual labour was mainly connected with agriculture ; and there is ground for believing that they were the best agriculturists of the period. Their example of peaceful toil had a beneficial influence upon the people.

Iona continued to prosper, and occasionally sent forth men of energy, who founded monasteries beyond the bounds of Scotland. In its day it performed good service, and contributed to the civilisation of the people. In spite of its solitary position evil days came upon it, for in 801 the monastery was burned by the Danes ; again in 806, they landed on the island and slew sixty-eight of the inhabitants ; and they returned in 815, and killed a number of the monks. By this time the influence of Iona had from other causes begun to decline, and ere the end of the ninth century Dunkeld had become the chief religious centre.

The influence of the early saints and their imme-diate successors upon the subsequent religious feelings of the people was remarkable, for till the Reformation their deaths and miracles were continually comme-morated as part of the worship of the nation. Their shrines and relics became objects of extreme vene-ration, and some relics were believed to possess marvellous powers. They took an extensive hold on local history and the nomenclature of the country ; the old markets all over the kingdom were named after them ; the wells, the caves, the rocks, and the moun-tains, often bear traces of the early saints. The new religion tended to draw the people more together, and contributed greatly to develope the unity of the nation

III.

STATE OF THE COUNTRY TO THE END OF THE ELEVENTH CENTURY.

AFTER the historic kingdom was founded, and while its development was proceeding from the centre outward, it was persistently attacked by external enemies. The Danes and Norwegians, under the name of Norsemen, threatened its total overthrow. Though these struggles cannot be fully detailed in this volume, it is requisite to mention them. Thus there were an internal and an external conflict going on at the same time.

Kenneth McAlpin died in 860, and was succeeded by his brother Donald, who reigned four years. Constantine I., a son of Kenneth, then ascended the throne, and had to struggle against the Norsemen. In the middle of the ninth century these ruthless warriors extended their destructive ravages along the east and west coasts of Scotland; they entered by the firths and inlets, and penetrated far into the interior of the country, ransacked it on every side, inflicted much suffering and privation on the people, and prolonged the reign of confusion. They obtained a footing in Caithness, Sutherland, and other parts along the coasts, where they established lasting memorials of their prowess in the memory of succeeding generations.

In 877 Constantine I. was slain in a conflict with the Norsemen on the coasts of Fife. Toward the end of this century they advanced into the heart of the kingdom, and in 900 King Donald, when fighting against them, was slain at Dunnottar. Constantine II. then mounted the throne ; and in 904 he defeated the Norsemen and slew their leader in Strathern. In 906 the king held a national council on the Mote Hill of Scone, in which the bishop and the people vowed to observe the laws and discipline of the faith. Constantine retired to the monastery of St. Andrews in 943, and Malcolm I. succeeded to the throne. He attempted to extend the bounds of the kingdom beyond the Spey, but failed ; and after a reign of eleven years, he was slain at Fetteresso, in Kincardineshire.

Indulf, a son of Constantine II., ascended the throne in 954. He took Edinburgh and added it to the kingdom In 962 he disappeared from the scene, and a contest for the throne arose between Duff and Colin, which terminated on the death of the latter in 971. Kenneth II., a son of Malcolm I., then succeeded to the throne. He immediately threw up entrenchments at the fordable points of the river Forth, and endeavoured to extend the kingdom southward. He invaded Northumberland, and struggled hard to consolidate the kingdom. After a reign of twenty-four years, he was slain at Fettercairn, in Kincardineshire.

Constantine III. mounted the throne, but his right was contested by Kenneth McDuff; and after a struggle Constantine fell in the second year of his reign. McDuff reigned eight years ; and was slain in Strathern. He was succeeded by Malcolm II., who ascended the throne in 10c5.

Malcolm II. began his reign by an invasion of Northumberland ; but he was defeated, and many of his followers were slain. He next attempted to extend his influence over the northern region of Scotland by the marriage of his daughter with Sigurd, the ruler of the Orkney Islands. In 1018 he mustered his army and again invaded Northumberland. A battle was fought at Carham, on the banks of the Tweed ; and Malcolm gained a complete victory ; a multitude of the enemy perished in the rout. The result of this battle was the cession of Lothian and the territory up to the Tweed. In his reign the kingdom of Strathclyde was incorporated into Scotland ; and the kingdom had reached its permanent frontier on the south side, as it stood when the great struggle with England began two centuries and a half later. Malcolm died in 1034.

He was succeeded by a grandson, Duncan, but other aspirants to the throne disputed his right ; and he soon became involved in a contest with the local chiefs beyond the Spey. After a severe struggle, Duncan was slain by Macbeth, near Elgin. Macbeth, the local chief of Moray, then advanced southward and mounted the throne, and for five years reigned in peace. In 1045 the adherents of the late king attempted to drive him from the throne, but he utterly defeated them. He was an able and vigorous ruler, and the kingdom enjoyed unusual tranquillity under his sway.

The late King Duncan left two sons, and their mother was a sister of Siward, Earl of Northumberland. The eldest son Malcolm, with the assistance of his uncle, collected an army in 1054, and marched northward to attack Macbeth. A battle ensued around the hill fort of Dunsinnane, where Macbeth had taken up his position, but the action was not decisive. The war was carried beyond the river Dee. On the 15th of August, 1057, Macbeth was defeated and slain at Lumphanan, in Aberdeenshire. The contest was continued by Lulach, the local chief of Moray, who was killed in Strathbogie, the following spring.

Thus Malcolm III., called Canmore, obtained the kingdom, and mounted the throne in 1058. He attempted to extend his power over Northumberland and Cumberland—districts which had been the scene of many contests for centuries, and were not as yet incorporated with England. One effect of the Norman Conquest of England was to drive a number of the Saxon people northward into Scotland. In 1067 Edgar, the heir of the Saxon line of kings, his mother and his two sisters, came to Scotland, and were welcomed by Malcolm. He married Margaret, one of Edgar's sisters, and hence became much interested in the claims of the Saxon prince.

Malcolm III. lent his aid to the disaffected chief of the north of England ; and he invaded Northumberland five times. In the last of these, when attacking the Castle of Alnwick, he was slain along with his eldest son on the 13th of November, 1093 ; and thus ended his reign of thirty-five years. At his death Malcolm left five sons—Duncan, the eldest by his first wife ; by Margaret, his second wife, Ethelred, who was lay-abbot of Dunkeld, and Earl of Fife ; Edgar, Alexander, and David. But Donald Bane, a brother of Malcolm III., claimed the throne, and a conflict arose between him and Malcolm's sons.

On the death of Malcolm, Donald Bane immediately took possession of the kingdom, and held it for six months, when he was driven out by Duncan, Malcolm's son. After a reign of six months Duncan was slain ; and Donald Bane again mounted the throne, and reigned three years and a half. But in 1097, Malcolm's eldest son by Margaret, Edgar, was placed on the throne, by the aid of a Saxon army led by his uncle ; and he reigned nine years and five months.

In the preceding pages I have briefly indicated how the historic kingdom was gradually developed outward from Scone and the banks of the Tay. It was at a later period that Edinburgh became the centre of government ; it never was the centre of the kingdom. At the end of the eleventh century the Celtic race occupied the greater part of Scotland. There were Saxons in the south, and along the eastern coast, and in the course of five centuries of contact they had partly commingled with the Celtic people, though not so completely as to sink their own language and customs. It was different in the west of Scotland and in the Western Islands.

where great numbers of Danes and Norwegians were absorbed by the Celtic race, and their language continued in these regions.

Only a brief reference to early Celtic art can be given. A few vestiges of primitive church building still remain in the Western Islands. The round towers of Brechin and Abernethy present an interesting type of early architectural structure. They show a striking resemblance to the round towers of Ireland. The round tower of Brechin stands at the south-west angle of the church, but was originally separate from it. The chief characteristic of Celtic art is its elaborate and beautiful ornamentation. This feature appears on weapons and personal ornaments and other objects. The peculiar style of ornament occurs on the early sculptured stones of Scotland. This class of monuments is chiefly found to the north of the Tay, and is believed to belong to the eighth, ninth, and tenth centuries.

IV.

THE NATION IN THE TWELFTH AND THIRTEENTH CENTURIES.

THE Norman conquest of England had the effect of
forcing a number of Saxons into Scotland, and a little
later a small number of Norman nobles frequented
the court of the Scotch kings, and received many
grants of land by charter from the Crown. In this
way legal feudalism was slowly introduced and spread
over the kingdom, though it was long and bitterly
opposed in some parts of the country. But before
the end of the thirteenth century feudalism was established in the Lowlands ; and Lowland Scotch—
an English dialect—was gradually encroaching on the
Celtic tongue. This dialect appeared in Lothian and
the south-east in the sixth century, and spread round
the north-east coasts as the Celtic language receded ;
and this change of language would have proceeded in
Scotland though there had been no Norman conquest
of England.

On the death of King Edgar at Edinburgh in 1107
his brother, Alexander I., succeeded to the throne ;
while his younger brother, Earl David, claimed the

portion of the kingdom which lies to the south of the Firths of Forth and Clyde. This arrangement continued during the reign of Alexander I. Shortly after his accession the king had to face a rising of the northern inhabitants, which he boldly met and suppressed.

COINS OF ALEXANDER I.

The relation of the Crown and the Church was then closer than in modern times, and one of the king's first acts was to nominate a bishop for St. Andrews. In 1107 he appointed Turgot, a monk of Durham, to the see, and immediately the Archbishop of York claimed a right to perform the ceremony of consecration, but the king and the Scotch clergy maintained that he had no authority over St.

Andrews. At last a compromise was effected, leaving
the disputed point unsettled ; and in 1109 Turgot
was consecrated by the Archbishop of York. The
new bishop did not find himself happy in the See
of St. Andrews, and he threatened to go to Rome
and settle all difficulties, but he died in 1115.

The bishopric remained five years vacant, but in
1120 the king nominated Eadmer, a monk of Canterbury, who was elected by the Scotch clergy and the
people. The point of consecration was revived, but
this time the Archbishop of Canterbury claimed the
right to perform it. Eadmer thought that the rights
of his mother church extended over all the British
Islands ; but the king rejected this view, and declined
to listen to it. The monk was as determined as the
king, and at last he declared, " Not for all Scotland
will I renounce being a monk of Canterbury." As he
could not agree with the king nor the people, he left
St. Andrews and returned to his mother church. In
1123 Alexander appointed the Prior of Scone to the
See of St. Andrews, but the king died before he was
consecrated. In 1128 the ceremony of consecration
was performed by the Archbishop of York, and there
was an express condition which reserved the rights
of both sees. The claim of feudal lordship over Scotland had not yet arisen, but it is obvious that if the
dependence of the Scotch Church on the English
Church could have been established, it would have
affected the independence of the kingdom.

Alexander I. died in 1124, and was succeeded by
his brother, David I. The kingdom was again placed
under one head, and the era of the introduction of

Norman feudalism had commenced. A large part of Scotland as yet hung loosely on the central authority; the country beyond the river Spey was hardly under the Scottish Crown, and Galloway was rather a tributary than an incorporated part of the kingdom. The local chiefs were naturally averse to the planting of Norman nobles among them, though these adventurers were favourites at the Court of David I. During his government of the southern part of the kingdom he had made some progress in introducing feudalism by giving his new followers and favourites grants of land by charter, which dispossessed the real owners of the land. In 1130 the people of Moray, under their local chiefs, Angus and Malcolm, rose against the king. They advanced to Stracathro in Forfarshire, where the king's forces met them. Angus was slain and his followers were overthrown, but his brother Malcolm retreated and prolonged the contest for four years. In 1134 the king in person proceeded to the disaffected north, and with his army succeeded in overawing the local chiefs, and then proclaimed the province of Moray forfeited to the Crown. He parcelled out large portions of the land of Moray among the Normans and adventurers who followed his banner.

In 1135 Henry I. of England died, and bequeathed his dominions to his daughter; but Stephen, a nephew of the late king, contested her right to the throne, and he proved successful. David I. naturally supported the claims of his relative the queen, and led an army across the border. Many of the northern castles of England opened their gates to him; when he advanced to Durham, Stephen approached with a large army, and the two kings confronted each other for fourteen days, and finally concluded a peace. But David I., besides his obligation to support the queen's claim, had a strong desire to annex the northern counties of England, and some hope of succeeding to the throne of England himself. So early in 1138 he again led an army across the Tweed. The defenders of England mustered at Northallerton, planted their standard, and prepared for battle. On the Scotch side the Galloway men led the attack, and rushed with such force on the enemy that the front ranks reeled and were driven back in confusion. But the English, supported by their bowmen, re-formed, and after a severe contest the Scots were completely defeated and many of them slain. Peace was concluded the following year.

The remaining years of David's reign were devoted to the various reforms which he introduced into the Church and the government. He reorganised the external polity of the Church, encouraged to the utmost the settlement of a class of Norman nobles in his kingdom, and endeavoured to assist and protect the borough communities.

In his reign the Church of Scotland was brought into accord with the prevailing form of Christendom. He founded or reorganised most of the bishoprics and monasteries, and endowed them liberally; he was the first king in Scotland who enforced the payment of tithes. The division of parishes and a parochial organisation began to assume form. But the monastic ideal cramped the development of David's

reforms. The kings and the nobles granted much
land to their favourite churches and monasteries, with
all the rights then attached to it, and for several generations this tended to promote the prosperity of the
kingdom, as the monks were the best agriculturists
of the country.

All the education of the age was in the hands of
the Church. The chancellor of each diocese was
entrusted with the supervision of the schools within
his bounds. At this period there were schools in
Abernethy, St. Andrews, Berwick, Perth, Stirling,
Ayr, Aberdeen, and other places. The literature
of the learned and all official documents were written
in Latin ; the literature of the people consisted of
ballads and songs, traditional tales and legends,
which were orally learned and transmitted from
generation to generation with such additional varia-
tions as imagination and circumstances suggested
to the national mind.

Charters were first granted to monasteries and
churches as title-deeds of their lands. Then the
kings granted charters conveying lands to Norman and Saxon nobles with despotic powers over
the inhabitants on these lands. From this starting-
point legal feudalism was gradually developed in
Scotland into a system unsurpassed in any nation.
And from then till now its effects upon the people
have been felt, but it was most palpably apparent
in the power and lawlessness of the Scotch nobles,
and the consequent weakness of the central government of the kingdom.

As there were rights of property in land before the

COINS OF DAVID I.

era of granting charters, so the inhabitants of towns had their recognised customary rights long ere they received royal charters. The earliest charters of royal boroughs always implied the existence of a community, and the charters simply recognised towns which already existed. But the Crown charter conferred on the citizens of the boroughs special rights and privileges of trade, local organisation, and government. Berwick, Edinburgh, Perth, Stirling, and Roxburgh were amongst the earliest royal boroughs, but the greater number of the boroughs received charters from David I.

In the twelfth century the boroughs to the north of the Grampians were associated for trade purposes. In the south they had a union called the Court of the Four Boroughs, which included Edinburgh, Stirling, Berwick, and Roxburgh. The members of this Court exercised legislative and judicial functions, and it has been inferred that they framed the code called the Burgh Laws which was sanctioned in the reign of David I. It is the most complete of all the early fragments of our legislation. This union gradually extended, and in 1405 delegates from all the boroughs south of the river Spey were ordered to assemble once a year to treat on their common affairs. Under the name of the Convention of Royal Boroughs it still exists, though most of its powers have departed.

These trading communities continued, and struggled to develop their organisations, the industry and the commerce of the kingdom. They afforded a source of revenue to the Crown, and the citizens were generally loyal supporters of the throne.

4

This was the church-building era in Scotland, and and most of the remarkable abbeys and cathedrals were erected or begun before the end of the thirteenth century. Some of them were a long time in process of building, and exhibit features of various styles of architecture. The Abbey of Melrose shows these varied characteristics.

David I. died in May, 1153, and was succeeded by his grandson, Malcolm IV., a boy of twelve years. He was crowned at Scone, but shortly after there was a rising in Argyle and the west, and the war continued through the winter among the mountains. There was also great disaffection in Galloway, and the royal army was repeatedly repulsed ; but at last the local chief, Fergus, was subdued, and then Galloway was placed in a kind of feudal subjection to the Crown. Still the inhabitants for long after retained their own local laws and customs.

In 1161 the people of Moray revolted, as they resented the intrusion of foreign nobles placed amongst them by the government, and the new taxes thus imposed upon them. Malcolm marched into the province with an army, and removed many of the people from the land of their birth, and placed them in other parts of the country among the mountains.

Malcolm died in December, 1165, and his brother William the Lion, then mounted the throne. The Scotch kings had long desired to annex the northern counties of England, and the disaffection of Henry's own children presented an opportunity to William. But Northumberland and Cumberland were then naturally almost absorbed into England. In 1173

William led an army across the border and wasted the north of England. The following year he again invaded England. When amusing himself he was taken prisoner by a party of English barons, and his capture entailed serious disaster on Scotland.

Henry II. had now a chance of obtaining the feudal superiority over Scotland which he eagerly desired. So he demanded an unqualified admission of this, and William gave it as a ransom for his personal freedom; and five of the chief castles of

COINS OF WILLIAM THE LION.

Scotland were to be placed in Henry's hands. This treaty continued in force for fifteen years, and to the day of his death Henry II. evinced a desire to cling to its fulfilment. In 1189, Richard I. ascended the throne, and annulled all the concessions extorted from William by Henry; the Scots paid to England ten thousand marks of silver, and the independence of the kingdom and the castles were restored to them.

Internal conflicts in the kingdom continued. The

Norman settlers in Galloway were driven out and slain; and in 1175, the king entered it with an army and subdued Gilbert, the local chief. In 1179 William invaded the remote district of Ross, subdued it, and erected two castles to support his authority. From 1181 to 1188, the districts of Moray and Caithness were in revolt, and the local leader, MacWilliam, aspired to the throne of Scotland. In 1187 the king mustered all the feudal force of the kingdom and marched to Inverness, with the intention of pursuing his enemy into the remote parts of the Highlands. William remained at Inverness, and a part of his army proceeded in search of MacWilliam. They encountered him in the upper valley of Strathspey; an engagement ensued on a moor, and MacWilliam was defeated and slain. For a time peace was restored in the north. But in 1196 the king was again in Moray and Inverness extinguishing a rebellion; and in 1211, he was among the mountains of Ross suppressing a rising, which was terminated two years later, when its leader was taken and executed.

William's reign was marked by the progress of feudalism and an increase of the royal power. Charters had become necessary to prove the rights of property. He reigned nearly fifty years, and died in 1214; and was succeeded by his son, Alexander.

Shortly after Alexander II. ascended the throne, he joined the English barons against King John, crossed the border, and invested the castle of Norham. John was extremely wroth, and advanced to the north with a mingled host of mercenaries. Alexander withdrew, and John followed him toward Edinburgh, burning Roxburgh, Dunbar, and Haddington, in his march. Alexander encamped on the river Esk, a few miles south of Edinburgh ; but John was afraid to risk a battle, and retreated and burned the Abbey of Coldingham, and kindled with his own hands the house where he slept the preceding night, as the signal for the burning of Berwick.

The line of the marches between England and Scotland had become pretty well marked. In 1237 a definite arrangement was come to, and from that date the efforts to extend the Scotch frontier southward ceased. But in the north and the west, and in Galloway risings were still frequent. In 1222, the king invaded Argyle, subdued it, and placed a portion of it under feudal subjection to the Crown ; but the northern part of it remained under the Lord of Lorne. The ultimate aim of the policy of the kings was to extend their authority to the utmost limits of the Highlands and Islands ; and in the midst of an expedition with this object, Alexander II. died in the Isle of Kerrera, on July 8, 1249.

He was succeeded by his son, a boy of eight years of age, who was immediately crowned at Scone under the title of Alexander III. During his minority the nobles entered on the policy of faction and ambition which figured so darkly in the subsequent history of the kingdom. The chief parties were the nobles of the north and west, the most potent of whom was Comyn, Earl of Menteith. The Comyns were a numerous and united group, and

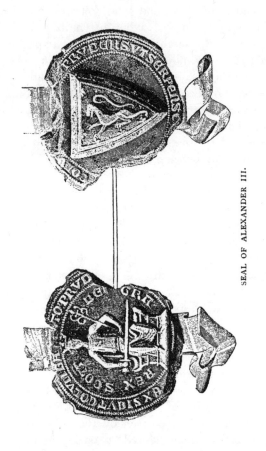

SEAL OF ALEXANDER III.

many of the old Scotch chiefs adhered to them ; the other party were mostly connected with the south of Scotland, and their foremost men were Alan Durward, justiciar of the kingdom, the Earl of March, and the Steward of Scotland. The latter party at every turn showed a desire to forward the interest of the kings of England, in the hope of thereby securing their own hold upon the land of Scotland.

The repeated attacks of the Norsemen were noticed in the preceding pages. The Islands of Orkney and Shetland were dependencies of Norway —ruled by a local chief ; the Western Islands were also claimed by her ; and on the mainland, to the north-west of the Moray Firth and Glenmore, there was a region forming a kind of debateable land, which the kings of Scotland had been long attempting to subdue. When Alexander III. attained the age of twenty-one he announced his intention to subject the Western Isles, and the war was commenced by the local chiefs of Ross. But Haco, the king of Norway, considered this pressure on the Western Isles as an encroachment on his rights, and prepared for war. In July, 1263, he embarked for the Orkney Islands with the most powerful armament that had ever steered from the ports of Norway. He plundered several places in his course, and the main fleet anchored in the Firth of Clyde between the Island of Arran and the coast of Argyleshire. The Scots proposed and obtained a truce, with the aim of gaining time, and when winter approached it was ended. The elements of nature were unfavourable

to Haco, and a tempest arose and disabled his great
fleet. Some of his ships were stranded near the
village of Largs, while the heights above the shore
were crowded with the Scots, ready to attack the crews.
Next day Haco landed with a strong reinforcement,
to bring off his men from the shore, and a sharp
engagement ensued. The Norwegians fought bravely,

COINS OF ALEXANDER II. AND III.

and at last the remnant of his stranded men gained
their ships. Haco, in a few days steered for Orkney ;
and on the 15th of December, 1263, he died.

When the tidings of his death reached the government of Scotland, it was immediately resolved to
reduce the Western Islands to subjection. Alexander III. sent an army into the Isles, and the local

chiefs were expelled, slain, and hanged; and the Earls of Mar and Buchan, and Alan Durward, returned with the spoil of the Islands. In 1266 a treaty was concluded with Norway, which ceded to Scotland all the islands off the coasts of North Britain; but the Orkney and Shetland Islands remained attached to the Crown of Norway till toward the end of the fifteenth century.

The remaining years of Alexander's reign were peaceful. He had a son and a daughter, both married, and the prospects of the nation were exceedingly bright; but they both died within a few weeks of each other, and left the king childless. The difficulty was at once seen, and a national council was immediately summoned. It assembled on the 5th of February, 1284, and there were present twelve earls, eleven bishops, and twenty-five barons, and they bound themselves in the name of the nation to support the right of the king's grand-daughter, Margaret, the Maid of Norway, as the heiress of the Crown of Scotland.

On the 15th of March, 1286, when the king was riding in the night along the coast of Fife, near Kinghorn, he was thrown from his horse and killed. A sad and mournful end; the lamentation was universal, and all looked forward to the future with dismay. The last king of the Celtic race slept with his fathers, and the Crown of a far-descended line fell to a weakly infant.

A meeting of the nobles and clergy was held at Scone, on the 2nd of April, 1286, when six guardians were elected to govern the kingdom. Several of the

SEALS OF DAVID I. AND ROBERT I.

nobles aspired to the throne, which they considered vacant. Robert Bruce entered into a bond with a number of Scotch and English nobles for the purpose of supporting his own claim to the Crown. It is uncertain whether Edward I. knew of this; but he had a project of his own. He had a son, and if his son could be married to the Maid of Norway, he imagined that all would go right. He therefore applied to the Pope to sanction the marriage of the two children; and a papal bull authorising it was issued in November, 1289. A treaty between England and Scotland was concluded at Brigham, in March, 1290, which sanctioned the marriage of the royal children. In this treaty the complete independence of Scotland was fully recognised and strictly guarded.

Edward I. quickly equipped a ship to transport the young queen from Norway. In due time the ship sailed from Norway with the queen on board. He despatched agents to Orkney to meet her, and sent jewels into Scotland to bedeck her. But the child died just before she reached the Orkney Islands, in September, 1290; and thus perished the hopes which Edward had associated with his marriage project.

V

WAR OF INDEPENDENCE.—WALLACE AND BRUCE.

THE nation then found itself without an heir to the throne in the direct line of succession. The chief nobles who aspired to the Crown were eagerly looking for supporters ; but the king of England had resolved to decide the fate of Scotland, and the current of events seemed favourable to him. On the first rumour of the queen's death the Bishop of St. Andrews sent a letter to Edward I., suggesting his interference in the affairs of Scotland, and this was the only invitation that he got to settle the succession to the Crown. Indeed, Edward I. had already formed his scheme, chosen his own path, and directed his energy to its accomplishment with great deliberation.

He issued writs commanding his barons to attend him at Norham on the 3rd of June, 1291 ; thus he prepared for any emergency which might arise ; while he invited the Scotch nobles and clergy to a conference at Norham on the 10th of May, to which they agreed. The conference was opened by an address from the Chief Justice of England, in which his lordship strongly asserted that Edward I. was the Overlord of Scotland, and, therefore, he appealed to the Scots to acknowledge this, that the settlement of the great matter before them might be facilitated. The Scots replied that they were not aware if such a right of feudal superiority belonged to him, and requested time to consult with the absent nobles and the community of Scotland, before giving an answer ; and three weeks were allowed to them, and then all were to reassemble at Norham. A clear answer was to be given on the question of the superiority of Edward I., and all those opposing it were requested to produce the documents or other evidence on which they founded their objections.

At the appointed time the meeting assembled on a green plain opposite the castle of Norham : eight claimants for the Crown of Scotland, and many of the Scotch nobles and clergy appeared. The Bishop of Bath began the business by reading the king's speech, which, after referring to the unhappy state of Scotland, proceeded, in a fine flowing style, to characterise the benignity of the prince who had come to her rescue. He then said that his master had allowed three weeks to the nobles and clergy of Scotland to bring forward whatever they could to impugn King Edward's right of superiority over that kingdom, and they had adduced nothing to invalidate it. But, in connection with this emphatic statement, one important fact has recently been brought to light, for a contemporary record proves that the community of Scotland lodged an answer in writing against Edward's demand of feudal superiority ; although it was not deemed relevant by Edward,

as it was more convenient for him and the claimants
of the Crown to ignore the people. Thus, when all
disturbing questions were brushed aside, Edward
announced that his title of Lord Superior was undisputed, and therefore he intended to act in that
character. Robert Bruce was asked whether he was
willing to prosecute his claim to the Crown of Scotland in the Court of the Lord Superior; and Bruce,
in the presence of the meeting, expressly recognised
Edward as Lord Superior, and agreed to abide by
his decision. The same question was put to each
of the claimants, and they all consented, without
reserve to the demand of Edward, and immediately
sealed their consent by letters patent.

Edward I. quickly followed up this recognition of
his power. He exacted the oath of allegiance from
all the Scots at the meeting; he commanded that all
the castles in the kingdom should be surrendered into
his hands; he reconstituted the government of the
country; the old seal of Scotland was broken into
four pieces, and a new one made, more suited to the
circumstances. A herald then proclaimed the peace
of King Edward, as Lord Paramount of the
Realm.

He next commanded the Guardians of Scotland
to exact the oath of allegiance to him as Lord
Superior of the Kingdom. Stations were fixed
where attendance should be given, and the swearing-
in process began on the 23rd of July, 1291, and was
continued for fifteen days. Edward himself visited
various stations, proceeding by Edinburgh, Stirling,
Dunfermline, Kinghorn, and St. Andrews, and

called upon all ranks to sign the rolls of homage as the vassals of their Lord Superior. All who were refractory were coerced by imprisonment and other punishments.

In 1291 eleven meetings were held, and at the last one, in August, Edward intimated that Bruce and Baliol should each select forty men as commissioners, while he should choose twenty-four or more if he thought fit, and these men were to meet in a body and consider the claims of the candidates for the Crown. At this meeting twelve candidates appeared and entered their claims; and Edward requested the commissioners to consider them all attentively, and report to the next meeting, to be held on the 2nd of June, 1292. But none of the candidates affected the current of history, except Bruce and Baliol, and to enter minutely into the details of the scramble would be foreign to the aim of this volume.

When the commissioners reassembled, the proceedings which followed present the air of an admirable piece of acting. The king first asked the Scotch commissioners to inform the Court by what laws and customs judgment should be given. They answered that, owing to difference of opinion among themselves and the importance of the cause, they were unable to come to a conclusion without deliberation, and therefore they sought the opinion of the English commissioners; but they also declined to commit themselves till enlightened by an English parliament. Edward then adjourned the meeting to the 15th of October, 1292, and declared that meanwhile he would consult the learned all over the world.

Many meetings were held before the final decision was announced. Bruce and Baliol argued their pleas at great length. When it became evident that Baliol would be preferred, Bruce presented a second claim for a part of the kingdom, and John de Hastings put in a similar one : these two in turn pleaded that the kingdom ought to be divided into three parts, and insisted that Scotland was partible like any other feudal fief. But the most peculiar feature of the proceedings was the complete elimination of any reference to the people of Scotland. It seems never to have occurred to the grasping claimants that there lived amongst the valleys and mountains of Scotland a strong-willed race, habituated to independence and freedom, whose spirit must be broken ere even the decision of the great Lord-Superior could be of much avail.

On the 17th of November, 1292, in the castle of Berwick, Edward, before a large assemblage, delivered judgment in favour of Baliol. The vassal king then rendered homage to his superior, and orders were issued to invest him in his fief. Baliol proceeded to Scone to be crowned, with a warrant from his Lord-Superior authorising the ceremony which was accordingly performed on the 30th of November. Shortly after he passed into England, and there concluded the last act of the drama by rendering homage to Edward I. as the invested king of Scotland.

When Baliol returned to his kingdom he found himself among a people little disposed to submit to him or his Lord-Paramount. If at any moment he had fancied himself fortunate in acceding to the throne of Scotland he was speedily and rudely disabused. It does not appear that he was gifted with much talent, but he was thwarted at every turn as an unwelcome master. Indeed it was rumoured that the poor man was in terror of his life, as he was now far away from his great lord and benefactor.

The Lord-Superior soon had an opportunity of exhibiting his power ; and he placed the vassal king in a most humiliating position. It had become known that the King's Courts were no longer supreme, as there was a higher authority which might reverse their decisions. A citizen of Berwick appealed to the Court of Edward I. against a judgment of the late guardians of Scotland ; and it was followed by another, touching lands of the Earl of Fife, on which the Scotch Parliament had given a decision, and Macduff, the defeated party, appealed to the Lord-Superior. Edward made it a condition that the king of Scotland must appear' as a party, and he was summoned to the Bar of the House. Baliol was insulted before the English Parliament as a contumacious offender, who had failed to show due respect to this august assembly : accordingly it was proposed to deprive him of the means of wrong-doing by taking three of the chief castles of Scotland into the hands of the Lord-Superior, until his vassal, King John, should render proper satisfaction.

In 1294, a quarrel arose between the king of France and Edward I., and war was declared. Edward summoned King John and the Scotch nobles to join his army ; but instead of obeying they held a parlia-

5

ment and dismissed all the Englishmen from the
Court ; and appointed a committee of twelve members
to conduct the government of the kingdom. The
position of the nation was rapidly becoming perilous.
In 1295, a treaty with France was concluded, in which
Scotland and France agreed to assist each other
against England. Shortly after, the Scots made two
inroads upon the northern counties of England. But
some of the nobles had joined the English, while
many others only gave a wavering support to the
national cause. Thus, at the outset, the people were
placed at a disadvantage ; while Edward I. could
command a far greater number of fighting men, and
he acted with energy and decision.

Edward determined to pounce upon Berwick, then
the richest town in Scotland ; and in the spring of
1296 he marched northward with a well-equipped
army. The citizens naturally resisted his attack, but
they were soon overpowered, indiscriminately put to
the sword, and eight thousand of the inhabitants
ruthlessly massacred. The town was utterly ruined.
Baliol now renounced his allegiance to Edward I., and
declared war against him ; but he had little energy,
and he was placed in trying circumstances, so no
effective resistance was offered to the invader at any
point.

From Berwick Edward and his army proceeded
toward Dunbar, where a straggling Scotch force was
met and dispersed. The castles of Dunbar, Jedburgh,
Roxburgh, and others in the line of his march, were
surrendered to him. He reached Edinburgh on the
6th of June, attacked the castle, and shortly took it.

He continued his triumphal progress to Linlithgow and Stirling, crossed the Forth unopposed, and, proceeding by Perth, passed the Tay, and entered Forfarshire. At the castle of Brechin on the 10th of July, 1296, the vassal King John came to his lord like a criminal suing for mercy, and submitted to Edward's pleasure. Then the documents considered necessary to degrade and dispossess him were drawn up and signed, and Baliol and his son were sent into England prisoners. Edward advanced northward by Aberdeen, till he reached Elgin ; thence he returned by a higher route, calling at Rothes, Kildrummy Castle, and on to Brechin. When returning south he took away the Coronation Stone from Scone—the venerated Stone of Destiny—as he was extremely anxious to efface every vestige of the national and patriotic feeling of the Scots. He adopted measures for the government of the kingdom ; and having settled everything, he proceeded home with the Stone of Destiny as a memorial of his Conquest of Scotland and a suitable offering to Edward the Confessor.

The seemingly complete depression of the Scots under the heel of the invader was the result of easily-understood circumstances, which have already been indicated. Thus Edward I. obtained a footing in the kingdom through the disputed succession ; while many of the nobles who should have come to the front at this crisis as the natural leaders of the people, had joined the enemy, and left them helpless and forlorn. But the native race of Scotland keenly felt their position, and the demeanour of the English soldiers aroused their ire, hatred sprung up between them, and bitter strife reigned in the land. At this perilous moment a hero arose to fight the battle of suffering, freedom, and national independence.

Wallace belonged to the lower class of the Scotch nobles, one of those who had never sworn allegiance to Edward I. In his early years he was under the care of his uncle, an ecclesiastic in Stirlingshire, from whom he received the rudiments of a classical training ; afterward he attended a school in Dundee for two years. He was gifted with rare mental faculties, tall in stature, and a commanding presence; he was a military genius, with a remarkable force of moral character. He soon kindled in the heart of the nation an unquenchable spirit of resistance to oppression.

He began his public career by attacking outlying parties of the English, and his followers increased with his success. At length he ventured to assail the English Justiciar in his court at Scone : the Justiciar escaped with difficulty, and a rich booty and some prisoners fell into Wallace's hands. In a short time Edward's new arrangements were thrown into utter confusion. But when he was told of the rising in Scotland he could not believe it, because so many of the Scotch nobles were with himself or in prison : he never even imagined that the Scots might attempt to act without nobles, and this lack of foresight to estimate the spirit of resistance among the people proved to be the missing link in Edward's scheme of conquest. Bishop Beck was sent to Scotland to extinguish the rising ; but he soon had to beat a retreat and narrowly escaped with his life.

When Beck returned, Edward commanded the whole military force north of the Trent to muster and crush the rebellion. An army of 40,000 men entered Scotland, under Henry Percy, and marched through Annandale and on to Irvine, where Robert Bruce and other nobles were lying in arms. As usual they were wavering and undecided, and without striking a single blow they concluded a treaty with the English at Irvine on the 9th of July, 1297.

A copy of this treaty was sent to Wallace, who was then in the north organising an army in conjunction with Andrew Moray of Bothwell, and they disregarded it. Andrew Moray was working hard in the district of Strathspey enlisting men and instructing them. Wallace was working vigorously in the counties north of the Tay, where he soon organised an army. He then attacked the castles, and many of them soon fell into his hands. He had just begun the siege of the castle of Dundee when tidings came that the English army was marching on Stirling. Wallace at once saw his opportunity, ordered the citizens to continue the siege, and hurried off with his army to guard the passage of the Forth.

Wallace posted his men on the rising ground which commanded the bridge of Stirling. The English army, 50,000 strong, lay on the opposite side of the river. When the English general saw the position of his enemy he tried to temporise, and sent forward messengers of peace ; but Wallace knew well the advantages of his position, and told them that he had resolved on battle—" to set his country free." On the 11th of September the enemy began to pass over the

narrow bridge, when one half of the army had crossed
it ; Wallace, by a preconcerted movement, attacked
the English in the rear, and intercepted between them
and the bridge. When this was executed, the main
body of the Scots instantly rushed down and assailed
the forming lines of the English, and threw them into
confusion ; a panic seized the whole army, and a

THE OLD BRIDGE OF STIRLING.

headlong rout ensued. Many were drowned in the
river and slain in the flight.

This battle had the effect of clearing the country of
the enemy, and all the strongholds were recovered.
Wallace was anxious to promote peaceful industry.
A document, dated the 11th of October, 1297, was
despatched to Lubeck and Hamburgh in the names of

Andrew Moray and William Wallace—generals of the army of the kingdom and community of Scotland ; they thanked the friends of the country for their services which the state of the kingdom had prevented the due acknowledgment, and informed them that commerce with the ports of Scotland would now be restored : " As the kingdom of Scotland, thanks be to God, has been delivered by battle from the power of the English."

In the end of this year Wallace was chosen guardian of the kingdom and leader of its armies, in name of King John. Although his abilities and energy were undoubted, still there was little hope for the nation, because the state of society rendered his success almost impossible. With the king banished and many of the nobles directly opposing him, and others lurking out of the way, the feudal system of defence could not be effectively worked, as Wallace could not change the organisation of society in a day.

When Edward I. entered Scotland in June, 1298, with an army of 80,000 men, Wallace could not face it in the field. So he drove off everything which could be removed, and left the country behind him waste ; in this way he hoped to starve and weary out the enemy. For a time he seemed likely to succeed ; the English were beginning to suffer severely. At last, through treachery, Wallace was forced to give battle near Falkirk. And, notwithstanding the original skill and generalship which he showed in the disposal of his troops on this memorable occasion, the disparity of numbers in the opposing armies were too great, and his small army sustained a crushing defeat.

But Wallace retreated with the remnant of his force ; and Edward's victory was fruitless, as he was compelled to drag his starving host back to England.

Soon after the battle Wallace resigned the government of Scotland ; and from this time we hear little more of him, although he was in various ways striving to serve his country up to the hour of his apprehension ; he went to France in connection with the affairs of Scotland. John Comyn of Badenoch and John de Foulis were elected guardians of the kingdom. Edward I. was then much embarrassed by the demands of his barons touching the great Charter ; but he was still straining every nerve to crush Scotland. In 1300, he invaded the country with a great army, and took several castles ; but after a campaign of five months he returned home without achieving any important success. In the spring of the following year he again invaded the kingdom at the head of a large army; but the Scots retired and avoided a battle, and he did not venture to cross the Forth. He then held most of the country on the south side of the Forth ; the Scots had retained the northern division of the kingdom since the battle of Stirling Bridge; and in 1302 they were gaining ground on the south of the Forth.

When Edward I. was freed of his difficulties at home and abroad, in the spring of 1303, he led an army into Scotland with the determination to reduce it to subjection or render it a desert. The Scots were unable to offer effective resistance to this overwhelming force. So the invader proceeded through the kingdom till he reached Caithness ; thence he re-

turned south and established his head-quarters at Dunfermline, and remained there through the winter. The
government and officials of the kingdom surrendered
to him in the winter of 1304. The terms granted to
Comyn and the chiefs who then surrendered were,
that they should retain their titles and estates subject
to a nominal punishment—merely to show that they
were rebels received to mercy. After a long and

STIRLING CASTLE.

heroic defence the castle of Stirling surrendered on
the 24th of July, and the garrison which numbered
140 men, were despatched to England prisoners.

Touching William Wallace, Edward determined
that he must surrender unconditionally. Comyn and
the nobles who adhered to him interceded for
Wallace ; there is evidence that Edward was pressed
to offer terms to him, but he declined to listen to any
suggestion of the kind. Edward I. at Stirling openly

CORA LINN, NEAR THE SUPPOSED CAVE OF WALLACE.

promised special favours to any of the pardoned
rebels who should exert themselves to capture
Wallace ; thus he hunted the man who had never
sworn oaths of allegiance to him to break them again
like many others whom he had often pardoned.
What, then, was the offence which Wallace had
committed ? Simply this, he had openly stood up
and fought against the invader for the liberty and
independence of the home of his fathers.

Wallace was found in Glasgow, put in fetters, and
conveyed to London. Tried for treason, which he
never committed, condemned, tortured, and executed
with all the cruelties of the Norman law, in 1305, the
details of which shall not pollute the pages of this
volume. But it is certain that his unjust and cruel
death did not advance the end which it was intended
to serve. For the story of the heroic action and
deeds of Wallace was embalmed in the heart of the
Scottish people, and his memory was venerated till it
became the very idol of the nation. In the later part
of the fifteenth century blind Henry the Minstrel, in
his rhymed book of Wallace, embodied the current
notions and sentiments of the people touching their
greatest hero : and for three centuries it had an
unexampled popularity amongst the Scots. Many
of our later poets have paid homage to Wallace, and
a few lines from a living poet of the people may be
quoted :—

> " Hail to thee, mighty Wallace ! so grand is thy fame,
> That the lapse of six centuries but brightens thy name ;
> And when cycles and cycles of time may have fled,
> They'd but heighten the glory enwreathing thy head.

    *   *   *   *   *   *

When legions of foemen, like dire inundations,
Strove to blot Scotland's name from the roll of the nations,
Then did'st thou arise, as the tower of her might,
To rally her sons and to lead them to right—
And vowed to the Powers that are sacred on high,
For Scotland to conquer, or for her to die."

After twelve years of incessant craft and bloodshed, closing with the execution of Wallace, Edward I. fancied that his conquest of Scotland was complete. But a worthy successor to Wallace immediately appeared upon the scene, and the shattered king lived to see it all passing from his grasp.

The Scotch clergy had given Edward I. much trouble. Bishop Lamberton of St. Andrews and Bishop Wishart of Glasgow had repeatedly sworn allegiance to him, and had broken it and joined Wallace and the national party. In 1304 Robert Bruce and Bishop Lamberton entered into a bond, in which they agreed to consult together and aid each other, and at all times assist their friends against their opponents. The existence of this document became known to Edward I., and Bruce, when attending the English Court, was questioned concerning it ; he at once saw that his life was in peril, and one morning he mounted his horse and rode swiftly to Scotland.

Bruce arrived at Dumfries in February, 1306, when the English judges were holding their courts ; and he halted there to attend to his duties as a freeholder of the county, and Comyn was present on similar duties. Bruce and Comyn entered the Gray Friars convent to have a private interview, and their conversation waxed warm. Bruce referred to the miserable state of Scotland, once an independent kingdom, and

now nothing but a province of England. He then
proposed that Comyn should take his lands and help
him to be king; or if he preferred it, Bruce was to
take his lands and assist him to be king. Comyn
demurred, and professed loyalty to King Edward.
Bruce charged him with betraying important secrets
of his; their talk became bitter and hot; and Bruce
drew his dagger and stabbed Comyn. He turned
from the convent and rushed into the street shouting
for a horse! his friends asked if anything was amiss.
"I doubt," said Bruce, "I have slain Comyn." Instantly Kirkpatrick, one of his followers, ran into the
convent and slew the wounded man outright, and also
killed his uncle, Sir Robert Comyn.

Probably the murder of Comyn was unpremeditated.
Still it removed the only competitor for the throne of
Scotland whom Bruce had reason to fear. Bruce was
a grandson of the man who fought out the contest in
Edward's Court with the deposed Baliol. His own
father died in 1304, and he then succeeded to the large
family estates in England and in Scotland. He was
a young man, little over thirty years, and hitherto had
shown a rather vacillating character. He had always
looked forward to the crown of Scotland; but Comyn
at the time of his murder had a preferable claim
to it. There was also a tradition that Comyn was
descended from Donald Bane, a brother of Malcolm
III., which would have given him a great advantage
among the people in any struggle between the two for
the throne of Scotland. But Bruce had rashly committed himself, and could not recede; he had assassi-
nated the highest noble in the kingdom, stained the

altar with blood, brought down on his own head all
the terrors of religion, and the enmity of the kin and
followers of the departed earl.

Immediately after the tragic deeds, Bruce drove the
English judges out of Dumfries and across the border.
The news soon spread, the people assumed a threatening attitude, and many of Edward's officials fled from
the kingdom.   Bruce resolved on a bold step and
mounted the throne, and was crowned at Scone on
the 27th of March, 1306 ; but his followers as yet
were few.

When Edward I. heard of these events in Scotland
he was extremely wrath, and threatened dire vengeance.   Orders with a sharp ring were issued.   It
was proclaimed in all the cities and towns of Scotland,
that all those in arms against the king should be
pursued by hue and cry, from city to city, from county
to county, from place to place, and taken dead or alive.
All persons taken in arms against Edward I. were to
be hanged and beheaded ; and all in any way connected with the murder of Comyn were to be drawn
and quartered.   The implacable rage of Edward runs
through all the royal proclamations.   Another great
invasion of Scotland was resolved on, and the advance
army under Pembroke reached the doomed country
in the spring of 1306.   Edward I. braced up all his
remaining energy, and once more moved northward,
but his frailty rendered his progress very slow.

Bruce and his party found that they could not face
the English army.   But he imprudently allowed the
enemy to approach his small party ; and it was
attacked at Methven on the 19th of June, 1306, and

utterly defeated. Bruce himself narrowly escaped, while many of his followers were taken and hanged and quartered. Many Scotsmen were tortured and executed with all the cruel formalities of the Norman law of treason.

The desperate nature of the enterprise now appeared. Bruce and his friends soon began to feel the extreme miseries of their position. They were pursued as outlaws, and forced to betake themselves to the rocks and mountains, while his supporters all over the kingdom were hunted, captured, and doomed to destruction. Bruce himself had great difficulty in keeping out of the clutches of the emissaries of Edward, and the Comyns pursued him with the inflamed and bitter feeling of revenge. For a time he became a simple fugitive, and endured many privations ; but he had the genuine mettle in his constitution, and the hard training which he was compelled to undergo, ultimately developed a man of rare ability and character.

In the end of the year 1306, Bruce, with a few of his friends passed over to the small island of Rachin on the northern coast of Ireland, and remained there during the winter. He returned to the mainland of Scotland in the spring of 1307. He had now gained some experience ; and on the 10th of May, in a well-chosen position at Loudon Hill, in Ayrshire, he gave battle to the Earl of Pembroke. Bruce posted his six hundred spearmen, and coolly awaited the attack of the English cavalry. They advanced and charged, but the spearmen stood firm, the cavalry reeled and broke ; the earl was totally defeated, and

ROBERT BRUCE.

retreated to the castle of Ayr. Bruce's followers now began to have confidence in him, and from this time he gradually gained ground.

Edward I. by short stages had advanced within sight of Scotland, but the hand of the grim enemy was upon him, and on the 7th of July, 1307, he expired. Edward II., who succeeded, was weak and incapable as compared with his father ; and Scotland slipped out of his hands. He advanced to the out-skirts of Ayrshire, and without effecting anything of importance, he returned home. Bruce was slowly gaining ground, and step by step retaking the kingdom. In 1309, the Scotch clergy proclaimed their adherence to Bruce, which was a great accession of strength to his cause, as he was under the ban of the Pope for the murder of Comyn. The English were driven out of the castles one by one, and Bruce immediately demolished the most of them, to prevent the enemy from again seizing them.

In the autumn of 1310, Edward II. entered Scot-land with a great host, but Bruce avoided a battle. After driving off their cattle and sheep into the narrow glens, the Scots retired to the woods and mountains ; while the invading army advanced to Renfrew, looking intently for an enemy to conquer, but in vain. The English began to suffer for want of food, and without doing anything of the slightest moment, the army retreated to Berwick. Several subsequent expeditions came to a similar end. In the summer of 1311, the Scots invaded the northern counties of England, and levied money, and plundered the country.

6

At last all the castles had surrendered to Bruce
save Stirling, and in 1313, it was besieged by Edward
Bruce. The English governor of the castle agreed to
surrender it, unless it should be relieved before the
24th of June, 1314. As it was the most important
stronghold in the kingdom, if England was to retain
a hold of Scotland, she must relieve it. So another
invasion was resolved on, and vast preparations were
made for a great display of force. The feudal array
of England was called out, and levies drawn from
Wales and Ireland. Edward II. entered Scotland at
the head of the largest and best equipped army that had
ever marched from England ; it numbered one hundred
thousand fighting men, one half of them cavalry, who
were then considered the chief arm of strength.

The Scots made a supreme effort. Bruce ordered his
force to meet in the Torwood, near Stirling, and found
that he could only muster thirty thousand men, and
five hundred cavalry. He prepared to guard and strengthen his position to the utmost, and to fight on foot.
After a careful examination of the ground, he resolved
to dispose his army in four divisions : three of them
forming a front line inclining to the south-east, facing
the advance of the enemy ; the fourth division being
held in reserve and placed behind the centre, under
the command of the king himself. The formation of
the Scotch spearmen was a series of solid circles so
inclined in front as most effectively to resist the shock
of cavalry charges. The right flank of his line was
well protected by the rugged ground and by the broken
banks of the Bannockburn ; while his left wing was
admirably secured by pits and trenches, which effec-

tively limited the space for the movements of the enemy's cavalry.

On the 23rd of June, 1314, the enemy appeared, and attempted to throw a body of cavalry into the the castle of Stirling, but they were repulsed by Randolph, the Earl of Moray. The Scots made all the necessary arrangements for the battle, and passed the night under arms on the field. At daybreak the Abbot of Inchaffary celebrated mass on an eminence in front of the army. He then passed along the line, and in a few words exhorted the Scots to fight for their rights and liberty. The soldiers breakfasted, and placed themselves under their different banners in battle array.

The English began the battle by the advance of a body of lancers and archers under the command of the Earls of Hereford and Gloucester. The lancers charged at full gallop on the right wing of the Scots, commanded by Edward Bruce ; but the spearmen firmly withstood the impetuous onset of the enemy. The main body of the enemy advanced and charged the centre, which was under the Earl of Moray. For a moment his division appeared to be engulphed amid the seething mass of the English ; and the whole Scottish line was soon assailed and wrestling in a hand-to-hand combat with the enemy. The battle raged with the utmost fury. The English attempted by desperate charges, many times repeated, to break through the Scottish spearmen, but in vain. At this all-important hour they thought of the home of their fathers and their own native hearths ; and remembering too the many grinding injuries, galling outrages,

stinging insults, cruel and unmitigated suffering
inflicted upon them during long years of dire oppression, they repelled every attack with steady valour
and slew heaps upon heaps of their assailants.

The English bowmen were galling the ranks of the
Scotch spearmen. Bruce sent Sir Robert Keith with
five hundred cavalry round the Milton Bog to charge
the left flank of the archers, who, having no weapons
to defend themselves at close quarters, were
instantly broken and scattered in all directions.
In front the battle continued to rage with unabated
fury, but with obvious disadvantage to the English.

Seeing the enemy flagging, Bruce encouraged his
leaders to strive on, and assured them that the victory
would soon be won. He then brought up the reserve,
and all the divisions of his army were engaged. The
English fought bravely, making many, but unavailing,
attempts to pierce through the front of the spearmen,
and at every successive charge losing more men and
horses, and falling into greater confusion. Then were
heard afar the clashing and crashing of armour ; the
whizzing flight of arrows through the air ; the commingled shouting of the war cries ; and withal, the
agonising moans and groans of the wounded and
dying. Masterless horses were madly running hither
and thither, heedless of friend or foe. The ground
was streaming with blood, and strewn with shreds
of armour, broken spears, arrows, and pennons, rich
scarfs and armorial bearings torn and soiled with
blood and clay.

The Scots continued to gain ground, and pressed
with fresh energy upon the confused and totter-

ing mass of the enemy, rending the air with shouts of " On them ! on them ! they fall ! " The English gave way slowly along the whole line. Bruce perceived this, placed himself at the head of the reserve, and raising his war-cry pressed on with redoubled fury on the falling ranks of the enemy. This onset, well seconded by the other divisions, decided the fate of the day. The English broke into disjointed squadrons and began to quit the field. In spite of all the efforts of their leaders to rally them and restore order, they dispersed and fled headlong in all directions. King Edward stood gazing intently upon the scene around him, and remained on the fatal field till all was lost, and at last fled in utter bewilderment. The struggle was over, the enemy in flight, and the victory complete. Glory to the heroes who fought, and bled, and fell on Bannockburn ; while Scotsmen's blood runs warm, and human sympathies endure, the nation's heart will throb over the remembrance of Bannockburn.

Thirty thousand of the English fell upon the field, and the standards of twenty-seven barons were laid in the dust, and their owners slain. Two hundred knights and seven hundred squires were among the fallen. The prisoners consisted of twenty-two barons, sixty knights, and a multitude of the lower ranks. Though only two men of high degree were slain on the Scotch side, nearly four thousand of the rank and file fell on the field. Bruce showed a noble forbearance in the hour of victory, and treated his fallen enemies and the prisoners with respect and humanity. In this he exhibited a striking contrast to the cruel policy of the Edwards.

After the battle of Bannockburn, Bruce's chief aim was to bring the English Government to equitable terms of peace, but they refused to treat him as a king. The Scots resorted to a convincing mode of showing the advantages which they had gained ; they crossed the border in force, and plundered and wasted the northern counties of England. England became anxious for peace, but the Scots would listen to it only on the condition of the full acknowledgment of the independence of the kingdom. The English were still loth to recognise this, and Edward II. tried the weapons of spiritual warfare and applied to the Pope for a pacifying Bull, which was issued in the beginning of 1317. This document was addressed to the illustrious Edward, King of England, and the noble Robert de Bruce conducting himself as King of Scotland. It ordered the observance of a truce between England and Scotland for two years. But Bruce declined to observe it or to treat with the representatives of the Pope unless he was addressed as King of Scotland, and told them that he would listen to no Bulls until he had taken Berwick. He pushed on the siege of Berwick, and it surrendered in the end of March, 1318. The Scots then invaded Northumberland, and took the castles of Wark, Harbottle, and Mitford. Shortly after, Bruce and his followers were excommunicated, but owing to the national sympathies of the Scotch clergy, this had no effect in Scotland.

It was felt, however, that the attitude of the king and the nation toward the head of the Church was unsatisfactory. Many denunciatory edicts had been issued from Rome against Bruce and Scotland since he mounted the throne, and England had done all that she could to increase their number and to enforce them. The immaculate Edward II. pretended that he could not treat with an excommunicated man like Bruce without a papal dispensation. Thus obstacles were constantly thrown in the way of peace, and the policy of King Robert was hampered. It was resolved by parliament in April, 1320, to prepare an address to the Pope, and present to him the real state of the nation: it is a document of much importance, and the following passage touching Bruce and the rights of the people is exceedingly interesting : —

"But at length it pleased God, who only healeth wounds, to restore us to liberty from these innumerable calamities, by our most valiant prince and king, lord Robert, who for delivering of his people and his own rightful inheritance from the enemies' hands, has most cheerfully undergone all manner of toil, fatigue, hardship, and hazard. The Divine Providence, the right of succession, and the customs and laws of the kingdom which we will maintain till death, and the due and lawful consent and assent of all the people, make him our prince and king. To him we are obliged and resolved to adhere in all things, both on account of his right and his merit, as the person who has restored the people's safety, in defence of their liberties. But, after all, if this prince should leave those principles which he has so nobly pursued, and consent that we or our kingdom be subjected to the king or people of England, we will immediately endeavour to expel him as our enemy, and as the subverter of both his own and our rights, and will choose another king who will defend our liberties ; for as long as one hundred of us remain alive, we will never consent to subject ourselves to the English. For it is not glory, it is not riches, neither is it honour, but it is liberty alone that we fight and contend for, which no honest man will lose but with his life."

This spirited and constitutional address had an immediate effect at the papal court ; the severe measures against Scotland were suspended, and afterward the Pope consented to address Bruce by the title of the King of Scotland. Many attempts were made to treat with England for a final peace ; but the English Government still continued to instigate the papal court to renew its edicts against Scotland. Bruce, however, determined to bring the English Government to reason. In June, 1327, a Scotch army entered England on the western borders, plundered the country, and returned home with their booty. They immediately prepared for another expedition against the eastern counties, and the king at its head crossed the border and attacked the castle of Norham. Thus did Bruce by his energy at last compel the English Government to sue for peace on equal terms.

In January, 1328, the English Government framed and issued a document which recognised Scotland as an independent kingdom as it stood in the reign of Alexander III. Thereupon a treaty was drawn and concluded at Edinburgh on the 17th of March, and ratified by the English Parliament in May, the same year. The important point of it was this—" And we renounce whatever claims we or our ancestors in bygone times have laid in any way over the kingdom of Scotland."

Robert I. had now secured the independence and liberty of the nation. . For this he had struggled more than twenty long years; sometimes standing alone while his nearest kindred and his followers fell captives and victims to the implacable rage and ambition of the enemy. Still, for all that he had suffered, he was forgiving and generous to his opponents, and he rarely abused a victory. He ruled the kingdom with much sagacity and wisdom, and enrolled the humblest class of the people in his army. He was kind and liberal to the poor and helpless, and withal one of nature's noblest sons. He died on the 7th of June, 1329, at Cardross, on the northern shore of the Firth of Clyde, and was buried in the choir of the abbey of Dunfermline. A marble monument was placed over his grave ; but he left a nobler monument—an enduring impression on the hearts of the people and in the memory of succeeding generations.

VI.

STATE OF THE NATION TO THE DEATH OF JAMES I.

ROBERT I. was succeeded by his son David, a boy of eight years, who was crowned and anointed at Scone on the 24th of November, 1331. Under King Robert's settlement, Randolph, Earl of Moray, became regent, and while he lived the kingdom was governed well. But he died in July, 1332, just when new troubles were coming upon the nation; and the Earl of Mar, who was elected regent, utterly failed to master the difficulties which quickly gathered round him.

Assisted by England, Edward Baliol, a son of the deposed King John, claimed the throne of Scotland. He landed in Fifeshire in the summer of 1332, with a force of four hundred cavalry and four thousand infantry. Although there were two Scotch armies in the field to oppose him, the incapacity of the regent led to the ruin of one, and the inaction of the Earl of March to the disbandment of the other, without the striking of a single blow. Thus it happened that Edward Baliol was crowned at Scone, on the 24th of

September, seven weeks after his arrival in the kingdom. For the next seven years the nation was torn by civil war, instigated and supported by England. In this space of time the King of England in person led four invasions in succession into the kingdom, and took possession of a large part of the country.

Yet the national party, though sadly shattered, had one or two able and honest men amongst them. Sir Andrew Moray, of Bothwell, was elected regent ; a skilful leader and an upright man, who infused confidence in the ranks of the party. In 1335 he attacked, defeated, and slew the Earl of Athole, at Culben, in the west of Aberdeenshire. After struggling hard to drive the enemy out of the country, he died in 1338, and was succeeded by the Steward of Scotland, a grandson of Robert I. In 1337 Edward III. advanced his claim to the throne of France, and there he found a more tempting field for his inordinate ambition. When Edward Baliol was left to his own resources, his poverty and nakedness soon appeared. He was an object of suspicion and hatred among the Scots ; and he fled in terror from the kingdom in 1339, and became a pensioned dependent on England.

The regent besieged Perth, the headquarters of the enemy, and in August, 1339, it surrendered. Before the end of this year Stirling and all the castles north of the Forth were recovered ; but those of Edinburgh, Roxburgh, Jedburgh, Berwick, and others were in the hands of the English.

Edinburgh Castle was retaken in April, 1341. Truces were concluded, but the Scots were unable to observe them while the English held possession of districts in the south of the kingdom. In 1346 the king mustered an army at Perth, and marched southward, crossed the border, and advanced to the vicinity of Durham. On the 17th of October a battle was fought, the Scots were defeated, and the king and many of the nobles taken prisoners; but the Steward escaped with the remnant of the army. The king and the prisoners of note were conveyed to London and imprisoned. The Earls of Menteith and Fife were selected as traitors, and tried and condemned. Menteith was executed, but Fife's life was spared. The English followed up their victory, entered Scotland, and overran anew several of the southern counties.

The Steward was re-elected regent. At this time of panic and confusion he ruled with wisdom and firmness. In 1347 a truce was concluded between England and France, which included Scotland, and it was continued by renewals to 1354. The adjustment of the king's ransom was a most difficult matter. After many abortive attempts and much wrangling it was fixed at 100,000 marks, to be paid in ten yearly instalments of 10,000 marks, or £4,000 of modern money. The Scotch Parliament acknowledged it as a national debt, and it proved an enormous burden on the people, as they were already impoverished by a war of sixty years. As a security for the fulfilment of the agreement, many hostages were delivered into the hands of the English government, and a truce was to be observed till the ransom was paid. Under these onerous terms David II.

returned to Scotland in 1357. But owing to his disposition and habits he found little in his own kingdom to satisfy him ; and he frequently returned to England and entailed more annoyance and expense on the people. David II. had no children by his wife, and in 1363 he suggested to the Scotch Parliament that it should choose as his successor Prince Lionel, one of the sons of Edward III. ; but Parliament rejected his proposal with scorn. In 1366 he submitted other proposals inimical to the independence and unity of the kingdom, which Parliament threw out as intolerable and unworthy of consideration. Such a man was utterly unfitted to lead the nation ; but his end was approaching, and he died in 1371, having nominally reigned forty-one years.

The Steward, who had been twice regent, succeeded to the throne, and was crowned at Scone, on the 26th of March, 1371, as Robert II. He was a man of good judgment, and inclined to the paths of peace, if the state of the kingdom had permitted it. The truce with England was continued ; but the Scots could not refrain from driving out the invaders, and by a slow process, which extended over many years, they retook the conquered territory in the southern counties of the kingdom. The league between France and Scotland was renewed in 1371. France resolved to stimulate the Scots against England, and in May, 1385, a French force of two thousand men arrived at Leith, under the command of John de Vienne, Admiral of France. The French had the pleasure of a raid into England, and of wasting

Cumberland and Northumberland. But the French
and Scotch modes of warfare were so different that
disputes arose between the leaders. The French
commander insisted that they should face the
English in battle, and at once strike a blow; the
Scots said such an attempt would be disastrous.
The dispute waxed warm; the Frenchmen talked
contemptuously of the spirit of their allies; and they
were only silenced when taken to the top of a mountain and shown the strength of the enemy's force.

A truce was concluded between France and England in 1389, which was accepted by Scotland, and
continued by renewals to 1399. This cheered the
last days of the aged king, who had long desired
peace; and he died in April, 1390, and was buried at
Scone. He was succeeded by his eldest son, under
the title of Robert III. This prince was an amiable
man, and fond of peace, but he lacked the strength
of character to restrain the restless and lawless nobles.
His brother, the Earl of Fife, afterwards known as
Duke of Albany, who had acted as regent in the
later years of his father's reign, continued to wield
the chief authority, under the name of Governor of
the Kingdom. The Earl of Buchan, another brother
of the king, ruled the northern part of the country,
and earned for himself the name of "the Wolf of
Badenoch." Amongst other oppressive acts he took
possession of land which belonged to the bishopric
of Moray; for this he was excommunicated. But he
retaliated by advancing with a body of his followers
to Elgin, and burning the grand cathedral, the
chantry, and the city.

Shortly afterwards the Wolf's natural son, Duncan Stuart, led a party of his adherents across the mountains, and plundered the Lowlands. In 1392 the landed gentry mustered and met him at Gasklune, but he completely defeated them. The government ordered Duncan Stuart and his accomplices to be proclaimed outlaws, for the slaughter of Walter Ogilvy and others ; but it is evident that Duncan Stewart was not harmed, for in subsequent history he reappeared as the Earl of Mar. The weakness of the Crown and the lawlessness of the nobles were the most striking features of the period.

The king, instead of being in a position to accuse the chief offenders or the administrative officials ot the Crown, was entering into bonds with the nobles for the protection of himself and his heir. Indeed, the weak monarch was reduced to the extremity of purchasing the favour of the nobles. The bonds between the king and his nobles assumed the form of annual grants of money, under the condition that they were to defend him and his eldest son ; thus he bound himself to give large sums annually to individual nobles for the natural period of their lives, and in some instances of the lives of their children. The Duke of Albany, Lord Stuart of Brechin, Lord Murdoch Stuart, Sir William Lindsay, Sir John Montgomery, and many others, were parties to bonds of this character with the king.

In 1398, owing to the infirmity of the king, Parliament appointed his eldest son, the Duke of Rothesay, Lieutenant of the Kingdom, with regal powers for three years. Rothesay was a somewhat thought-

RUINS OF ST. ANDREWS CATHEDRAL.

less young man, impatient of opposition, yet open and courageous, and not beyond hope of improvement under the sobering effect of experience. But his uncle Albany, the late governor, was an ambitious man, fond of power, and cold and pitiless. Their position made them enemies of each other ; and Albany formed a plot against the young prince, who was unable to cope with his unscrupulous relative. The Earl of Douglas and others joined Albany, and means were soon found for executing their dismal design.

The Bishop of St. Andrews died in 1401. It was customary for the castle of a deceased bishop to be occupied by the Crown till the election of a new one. With this idea in his mind Rothesay was proceeding to occupy the castle of St. Andrew's, and when within a mile of it he was arrested, conveyed to the castle of Falkland, and imprisoned. A few weeks afterwards his body was removed, and interred in the monastery of Lindores, and a report issued that he had died of a bowel complaint. But the people asserted that he had been murdered—by the cruel mode of utter starvation. There was the usual farce of a parliamentary inquiry into the cause of his death, in which it was gravely stated that he died by the visitation of Divine Providence, and not otherwise. Albany, Douglas, and their accomplices were indemnified, and every one was forbidden to spread false rumours against them. The aged and unhappy king bitterly lamented the fate of his son, but he was utterly powerless. On the death of Rothesay, Albany resumed his position as governor of the kingdom.

It was resolved that Prince James, the king's other son, a boy of fourteen years, should be sent to France for safety, and to complete his education. He sailed in March, 1405, and when off Flamborough Head he was captured by an English ship, conveyed to London, and lodged in the Tower. When his guardians remonstrated, Henry IV. replied that he knew the French language very well, and therefore his father could not have sent him to a better master. The Duke of Albany was rather pleased at the capture of the prince, and it was suspected that he had concerted it. After seeing the misfortunes of his family, Robert III. died on the 4th of April, 1406, having reigned sixteen years. Parliament recognised the captive Prince James as the heir to the throne. As next in the line of succession Albany was elected regent, and continued to rule the kingdom.

The Scots were gradually pressing the English out of the border counties. In 1409, the castle of Jedburgh was recovered, and, having been more useful to the enemy than to the Scots, was levelled to the ground. About the same time Fast Castle was retaken.

A truce was concluded with England in 1412. The Duke of Albany died at Stirling on the 3rd of September, 1419, at the age of eighty years. He had ruled the kingdom for thirty-four years, and his son, Murdoch Stuart succeeded to the office of governor. But he lacked the energy to pursue a line of policy like his father, and the kingdom under him soon presented a scene of anarchy.

Prince James began to make efforts to obtain his freedom. Negotiations were opened and a treaty was concluded in 1424. Scotland agreed to pay to England forty thousand pounds in annual sums of ten thousand marks. It was arranged that James should marry the daughter of the Earl of Somerset ; and the marriage was celebrated in Southwark amid great pomp. A truce for seven years was concluded. The King moved northward, crossed the border on the 1st of April, and was warmly welcomed by the people.

The return of James I. was an important event in the history of Scotland. He was crowned at Scone on the 21st of May, 1424. It soon appeared that a man of talent and energy was at the head of the government. James had resolved to humble the nobles and break their power. His plans were well conceived, and executed with striking energy.

He assembled a parliament at Perth on the 12th of March, 1425. For eight days it was engaged in passing laws against the diffusion of heresy, bands among the nobles, and the restoration of the lands of the Church which had been wrested from her and illegally possessed. On the ninth day the Duke of Albany, his second son, and a number of the chief nobles, were seized and imprisoned. Parliament was then adjourned. The Earl of Lennox and Albany's eldest son, Walter Stuart, had been previously arrested and imprisoned. A court was held at Stirling on the 24th of May. It began with the trial of Walter Stuart, who was accused of robbery, convicted, condemned, and immediately beheaded. The next day the king's own cousin Murdoch Stuart, Duke of Albany, his second son, Alexander,

INVERNESS FROM THE RIVER SIDE.

(*Present state.*)

and the aged Earl of Lennox, were tried, convicted, and sentenced to death; and they were all executed before the castle of Stirling. Albany and his sons were men of stalwart and commanding presence, and their fate excited much sympathy among the people. Indeed this action of the king, which flooded the scaffold with the blood of his own kindred, cannot be justified. Probably he intended to exhibit a striking example of severity; he may have wished the nobles to understand that a change had taken place in the government, and that the lawlessness which had prevailed, must henceforth cease.

James, having restored order in the Lowlands, directed attention to the Highlands and Western Islands, and summoned a parliament to meet at Inverness. In 1427, he proceeded to Inverness, and summoned the Lord of the Isles and fifty of the most notable chiefs to attend his parliament. They attended, and were instantly seized and imprisoned, and a number of them were executed. The Lord of the Isles was related to the royal family, and on making due submission, he was liberated. But he was displeased with the whole proceedings, and immediately after the departure of the king he mustered his followers and attacked Inverness. The king returned, and met him in Lochaber, defeated him, and pursued his retreating followers over the mountains and from glen to glen. At last the Lord of the Isles surrendered, and in 1429 he was imprisoned in the castle of Tantallon; but after a few years, he was liberated and restored to his possessions.

The chief aim of James I. was to make the nobles

more dependent upon the Crown ; to restrain them
from oppressing the people ; and to rule the kingdom
through Parliament acting with the executive power
of the Crown.   He attempted to introduce the
principle of representation in the election of members
of Parliament.   In his short reign parliament was
assembled fifteen times, and besides transacting other
business, his parliaments passed upwards of 160 distinct statutes, which were written and proclaimed in
the language of the people.   These Acts were brief,
incisive, and clearly expressed, and dealing with many
important matters, especially the reform of the
administration of justice.   It was commanded that
justice should be equally distributed in every part of
the kingdom, "to the rich as to the poor, without
fraud or favour."

He pursued his object of reducing the power of
the nobles with inflexible determination.   In 1431 he
ventured on an extremely bold step.   Parliament
had decided that the late governor, Albany, had
no power to alienate any lands which by the death
of a bastard might have fallen to the Crown, and
on this ground a grant of land to Adam Ker was
invalid.   In this way the king prepared for a great
stroke.   The Earls of March, who usually commanded
the castle of Dunbar, and held large estates in the
south of the kingdom, had long been a cause of annoyance to the Crown.   In 1401, the Earl of March joined
the English and fought against the Scots ; but he
returned to Scotland in 1408, and his estates were
restored to him by the Duke of Albany.   He died
in 1420, and his son George succeeded to the lands

of the earldom ; and it was this man that the king
resolved to humble. A parliament was assembled
at Perth in 1435, and proceeded to discuss the cause
of the earldom of March. It was debated on both
sides :—First, touching the treason and forfeiture of
the late earl, and the consequent reversion of his
estates to the Crown ; and second, the position and
claim of his son then in possession. The verdict of
the judges was against the earl, and all the lands of
the earldom were annexed to the Crown. The
dispossessed earl and his family retired to England.

About this time died the Earl of Mar, Duncan
Stuart, the outlaw and hero of Harlaw, mentioned
in a preceding page, and his estates reverted to the
Crown on the ground of his illegitimacy. The Scotch
nobles were now alarmed, and enraged at the
proceedings of the king ; and they formed a plot to
murder him. The chief actors in the dismal plot
were Walter Stuart, Earl of Athole, a son of Robert
II. ; Robert Stuart, a grandson of Athole's, who
was then chamberlain to the king ; and Sir Robert
Graham. Graham in parliament vehemently denounced the king for his encroachment upon the
nobles, and he was banished and his property forfeited. He then went to the Highlands and matured
the plot ; he renounced his allegiance, and warned
the king that he would pursue him as his enemy and
slay him.

James resolved to hold his Christmas at Perth, in
the Black Friars Monastery. Though he was solemnly
warned of his personal danger, he disregarded it.
Graham and his accomplices arranged to commit

their horrid crime on the night of the 20th of February, 1437 ; and Stuart, the chamberlain, re-moved the bolts of the doors which made commu-nication in the interior of the building easy.   The king had undressed, and was standing in his night-gown before the fire, talking with the queen and the ladies of the bedchamber, when he was alarmed by the clang of arms and the glare of torch-lights in the outer court.   The queen and the ladies rushed to secure the door, but the bolts were gone.   The king instantly saw his peril, and, seizing the tongs, wrenched up a flag and descended to a vault below.   The cruel ruffians rushed through the building and feared that their victim had escaped.   But Thomas Chambers suspected what had happened, and returned to the bedchamber, and seeing that the floor had been newly broken, instantly tore it up, and their victim appeared.   Sir John Hall leaped down, but the king seized him by the throat and threw him under his feet.   A brother of Hall's followed, and met the same fate.   Graham then sprang down with his drawn sword, and the king implored for mercy ; but Graham called him a cruel tyrant, who had never shown mercy to his own kindred, and in an instant thrust his sword through the king's body.   Thus perished, by the hands of atrocious villains, the ablest king of all the Stuart line.

VII.

CONFLICTS BETWEEN THE CROWN AND THE NOBLES.

AFTER the tragic end of James I., his son, a boy of eight years, succeeded to the throne, and was crowned in the monastery of Holyrood on the 25th of March, 1437. The custody and care of the prince was entrusted to his mother; and the Earl of Douglas was appointed Lieutenant of the Kingdom. During the minority the factions of the nobles struggled to kidnap the king. The queen with her son had taken refuge in the castle of Edinburgh, but the governor, Sir William Crichton, isolated the boy from his mother and made him a kind of prisoner. The queen outwitted him, and conveyed her son to Stirling Castle, which Sir Alexander Livingston commanded. In 1439, the queen married Sir James Stewart, the Black Knight of Lorn, with the hope of strengthening her position; but Livingston imprisoned them both, and kept the young prince a captive in Stirling Castle.

The Earl of Douglas died in 1439, and his son, a youth of seventeen years, succeeded to the earldom.

SOUTH SIDE OF EDINBURGH CASTLE. (*After Sleyer.*)

He kept a host of retainers, and scorned to appear at Court or parliament. The factions of Livingston and Crichton saw that the earl must be crushed. As they were unable to attack him in the field, they resolved to allure him into a trap. They invited him to visit the young king in Edinburgh Castle. The earl and his brother proceeded there, and were received with much show of respect. But in a few days after their arrival, they were both beheaded. This blow stunned the Douglas family. A portion of the estates of the earldom reverted to a sister of the murdered earl, while his grand uncle, James Douglas, succeeded to the title and the greater part of the lands. He died in 1443, and his son, William Douglas, succeeded. William was a man of energy and ambition. His power soon became enormous and inconsistent with order, and the kingdom presented a scene of turmoil. To make himself master of the kingdom, he sought admittance to the king's presence at Stirling Castle, and Livingston who had the custody of the prince granted the request. Livingston and Douglas became friends, and Crichton saw with dismay that he was undone. Douglas assumed the title and power of Lieutenant-general of the Kingdom, called a parliament and summoned Crichton and his adherents to appear and answer to a charge of high treason. Crichton, instead of obeying the summons, mustered his followers, plundered the lands of Douglas, then retired into the castle of Edinburgh, and defied his enemies. And they afterwards came to terms with him.

The Earl of Douglas divorced his wife, then

married his cousin, the " Fair Maid of Galloway,"
and thus reunited the domains of his house. His
power rapidly increased, and a struggle with the
Crown became inevitable. In 1449 the king married,
and began to show energy and ability, but he mainly
relied on the counsel of Crichton the Chancellor and
Bishop Kennedy. The king had not sufficient power
to attack Douglas openly, and so the faction of the
Livingstons were first crushed. The Livingston family
who had enriched themselves during the king's
minority, were seized and imprisoned. The head of
the house, an old man, was granted his life ; but his
son and several others of the faction were executed.

Douglas continued to hold a haughty attitude
toward the king, and it was proposed to try the effect
of a personal interview. In February, 1452, he was
invited to visit the king at Stirling Castle, and he complied. He dined and supped with the royal party,
and then the king took him aside to an inner room
where they entered into a private conversation. One
matter after another was touched on, till the question
of Douglas's bonds with the Earls of Crawford and
Ross was broached. Their talk waxed hot, the king
insisted that Douglas must break these secret bonds,
but he declined to desert his allies. At last the king
exclaimed, " This shall," and instantly drew his dagger
and twice stabbed his guest. The nobles at hand
rushed upon the bleeding man and killed him outright. There can be no justification or palliation of
this murder ; perhaps it was unpremeditated, as there
was no preparation made to meet its consequences.

The rash act of the king hastened the crisis, and

civil war raged from the borders to Inverness. The struggle was desperate, and the king was hard and sorely pressed. He appointed the Earl of Huntly Lieutenant-general of the Kingdom, and entrusted to him the task of suppressing the rebellion of the Earls of Crawford and Ross. Huntly, at the head of the royal army, attacked Crawford near Brechin, and, after a severe battle, defeated him. But Crawford retreated to Finhaven Castle, and continued to harass all whom he considered his enemies.

Huntly turned to chastise the Earl of Moray, who had invaded and wasted Strathbogie. He crossed the Spey, advanced into Moray, and destroyed one half of the city of Elgin. Thus the rebellion was subdued in the north. But in the south the war raged with intense fury. The new Earl of Douglas and his brothers defied and scorned the king's authority, and burned and wasted the country. At last the Earl of Angus, a member of the Douglas tribe, joined the king's standard. His kinsmen looked on this as an unpardonable crime, and attacked his possessions with extreme ferocity. After many fruitless efforts the king managed to muster an army, and advanced in person against the Earl of Douglas, entered his territory and proceeded through Peebles-shire, Selkirk Forest, Dumfries, and Galloway. Douglas Castle was captured, and peace was concluded in August, 1452. Douglas agreed to renounce his claim to the earldom of Wigton, and the lands of Stewarton, and to abandon all quarrels arising out of recent events and all illegal bonds.

But Douglas married his brother's widow, and once

more united the territories of the family. He entered
into communications with the Yorkish party in
England, and conspired to overthrow the Government
and the Stuart dynasty. An appeal to arms again
became necessary. The king raised an army, and
marched into the lands of Douglas, besieged and took
the castle of Abercorn ; and other castles of the rebel
chief soon fell into the hands of the king. Douglas
made a last effort at Arkinholm, but was defeated by
the royal troops under Angus. In this engagement
one of Douglas's brothers fell, and another was
captured and beheaded. Douglas himself fled to
England, and the estates of the earldom were forfeited
to the Crown.

England still retained Berwick and the castle of
Roxburgh, and the Government determined to take
the latter ; but it was strong and obstinately defended
by the English. In the siege of Roxburgh cannon
were used, and the king was present to urge on the
operations. One of the great guns was brought from
Flanders, and the king was eager to see the effect of
its working. When it was discharged some of the
wedges which were used to tighten the iron hoops
were driven out, and one of them struck and killed the
king. But the siege was continued, and the castle
taken. Having been more serviceable to the enemy
than to Scotland, it was levelled with the ground.

James II. was succeeded by his son, a boy of eight
years of age, who was proclaimed king at Kelso
under the title of James III. For several years the
government was conducted by Bishop Kennedy. He
died in 1466, and the usual plotting of the restless

nobles recommenced. The family of the Boyds entered into a bond with a number of nobles to support each other, to sieze the young king, and rule the kingdom in their own interest. So on the 19th of July, when the chamberlain was holding his court at Linlithgow with the king, Lord Boyd and a number of his associates entered the court, and requested the king to accompany them to Edinburgh, and of course he complied. Lord Boyd was then appointed guardian of the king's person, governor of the royal castles, and High Justiciar of the kingdom. Thus he at once became supreme, and his family and relations speedily acquired large tracts of territory. In 1467 Lord Boyd's eldest son was created Earl of Arran, and married to the king's sister.

It was stated in a preceding chapter that the Western Islands were ceded to Scotland in 1266, and the payment of an annual rent of 100 marks was one of the terms of the treaty. This had not been regularly paid, and the arrears amounted to a considerable sum. A marriage was proposed between James III. and a daughter of the King of Denmark, and the Earl of Arran and other commissioners proceeded there to negotiate it. They concluded a treaty with King Christian, in which he agreed to abandon his claims for the arrears of rent on the Western Islands ; to endow his daughter with 60,000 florins, of which he proposed to pay 10,000 florins before she departed to Scotland, and to secure the remaining 50,000 on the Orkney Islands. But on further reflection, he proposed to give the bride 2,000 florins for her immediate use

ARRAN.

and secure the balance on the Shetland Islands. The treaty thus adjusted was accepted ; and, as the money was never paid, the Orkney and Shetland Islands became incorporated with Scotland.

When the Earl of Arran returned with the king's bride, he found that his enemies had undermined his power and that he was utterly deserted ; and he immediately fled with his wife to Denmark. But he was soon stripped of his royal wife by a divorce. She afterward married the head of the Hamilton family, and this house subsequently attained a high position in the kingdom.

As the Boyds had risen rapidly, so their fall was equally swift and complete. In 1469, they were tried for treason and convicted. Old Boyd, the head of the house, fled to England, where he shortly afterwards died. His brother Alexander was executed on the Castle Hill of Edinburgh. The extent of the lands which they had unjustly seized in the short day of their power, is well shown by the local names in the act of their forfeiture. The lordship of Kilmarnock was the hereditary possession of the family, but the list in the act contained the lordship of Bute, the castle of Rothesay, the lordship of Arran, the earldom of Carrick, the lordship of Cowal, the lordship of Stewarton, the barony of Renfrew, and several others. The case of the Boyds is not an isolated one in our story, as a similar policy was pursued by the nobles whenever they had an opportunity. It was the chief source of their endless feuds.

James III. had attained his ninteenth year, and, as already stated, was married. But his education

had been sadly neglected, and he showed little capacity
in the government of his kingdom.   He was peace-
fully inclined and lacked the energy of character
necessary to control the nobles.   His two brothers,
the Duke of Albany and the Earl of Mar, perhaps
because they were active and popular men, the king
seems to have regarded as his enemies.   Mar died in the
castle of Craigmiller, and it was widely rumoured that
the king had caused him to be murdered.   Albany
was imprisoned in the castle of Edinburgh, but he
escaped and fled to France.   In 1482 he came over
to England, and entered into a treaty with the English
Government, in which he agreed to recognise the feudal
superiority of England, while the English king was to
give him the Crown of Scotland under the title of
Alexander IV.   Albany promised to render homage
to his feudal lord whenever he was put in possession
of the kingdom ; to support England ; and abandon
the old alliance with France.   The old Earl of
Douglas was still alive and a retainer of the English
king, and he and several other Scotch nobles joined
the plot.

Thus the relations of England and Scotland became menacing.   In July, 1482, an army was mustered on the Burghmoor, near Edinburgh, and with the
king at its head marched toward the border.   When it
reached Lauder a tragic action happened.   Cochrane,
one of the king's favourites, who had originally been
a mason, had charge of the artillery.   The nobles met
in a church, and resolved to sweep off the king's
favourites.   While they were talking a knock was
heard at the door ; it was Cochrane with a message

from the king. The Earl of Angus seized and pulled the gold chain from Cochrane's neck, saying that a rope would befit him better. "My lords," said he, "is it jest or earnest?" He was told it was earnest, and was quickly bound and placed under guard. A party of the nobles, who were despatched to the royal tent, instantly seized the king's musician, Rogers, and the rest of his favourites and servants. These were then led along with Cochrane to the bridge of Lauder, where they were all hanged.

After the execution of the favourites, the nobles disbanded the army and left the country a prey to the enemy. The English retook Berwick, which henceforth remained in their possession. The nobles imprisoned the king in Edinburgh Castle. The Duke of Albany came to Edinburgh with the English army, with the intention of mounting the throne. For a short time he ruled the kingdom ; but when his intrigues with the English Government became known in Scotland, he was forced to retire, and he finally settled in France.

The nobles, continuing to plot against the king, at last resolved to dethrone him. It occurred to them that the king's son, a youth of sixteen years of age, would serve their purpose, and the southern nobles induced him to join them and rise in rebellion against his own father. They mustered their followers and advanced upon Edinburgh. The king crossed the Forth and passed into the northern counties which were loyal, and there a strong force rallied round him. He then marched on Stirling, but the governor of the castle had joined the rebels. On the 28th of

June, 1488, the two armies approached each other at a small brook, called Sauchie Burn, in the vicinity of Stirling. An engagement ensued, and was fiercely contested. The king fled from the field. His horse stumbled and threw him, and some of the rebels came up and killed him. Thus fell James III. in the thirty-fifth year of his age and twenty-eighth of his reign, another victim to the ambition of a reckless aristocracy.

A few days after his father's death, James IV. was crowned at Scone ; and the faction who held the reins of government proceeded to make themselves secure. James IV. took an interest in shipbuilding, and in his reign the nation made some progress as a naval power. The relations of Scotland became more and more interwoven with the other kingdoms of Europe. Spain, then in the zenith of her glory and power, had an ambassador at the Court of Scotland. She was forming a league against France, and desired to sever James IV. from his old ally ; but in this she failed.

The internal state of England had for some time rendered her a quiet neighbour. In 1495, negotiations were begun touching the marriage of the king with the daughter of Henry VII. The treaty of marriage between James IV. and the Princess Margaret of England was concluded in January, 1502 ; and on the 8th of August, the marriage was celebrated in the chapel of Holyrood amid the rejoicing of the people. A hundred years later the issue of this marriage united the crowns of the two kingdoms.

JOHN, DUKE OF ALBANY, AND QUEEN MARGARET.

In 1509, Henry VII. died, and Scotland lost a quiet neighbour. His son, who succeeded, was a different personage, and shortly after his accession the old strife was renewed. England was entering on a war with France, in which Scotland was to take the side of her old ally. In the summer of 1513 the feudal force of the kingdom mustered on the Burghmoor; and, with the king at its head, marched to the border and crossed the Tweed on the 22nd of August. Much time was lost in attacking a few border castles, instead of advancing and striking a blow before the enemy was prepared to offer serious resistance. But the king, disregarding the counsel of the ablest men in Scotland, allowed the enemy to take every advantage. The battle of Flodden was fought on the 9th of September, 1513. James, whose idea was to have a stand-up battle, fought on foot with his own hand in front of the centre; and although his bravery was surpassing, it only increased the carnage, as the flower of the army crowded round him and fell in a hand-to-hand struggle with the enemy. The loss of the Scots was lamentable, upwards of eight thousand being left upon the fatal field, and among them the king. Indeed there was hardly a family of any note in the kingdom but had lost some of its members.

A glance may be taken here at the rise of the literature of the nation, and the institution of the Universities. Prior to the fourteenth century the national literature consisted of ballads and traditional tales. The early Scotch Chroniclers composed their narratives in rhyme. John Barbour's metrical story

of King Robert Bruce is the best extant specimen of the national literature of the fourteenth
century. He was writing it in the year 1375, and
the Government rewarded him with a pension "for
writing the Book of the Deeds of King Robert I."
Barbour died, at an advanced age, about 1396.
His book on Bruce has much literary merit and
historical value.

Andrew Winton, Prior of St. Serf's Monastery,
produced his Original Chronicle of Scotland in the
form of a metrical story. He was prior in 1395, and
lived to 1420. Winton commenced his Chronicle
with a history of the world, and treated of·angels, the
Creation, the death of Abel, the generations of Cain
and Seth, the primeval race of giants, the ark of Noah
and the Flood, and a long series of other topics. His
language is similar to Barbour's. The later portion
of his narrative is valuable, its simple account of
events being generally trustworthy ; and his descriptions are interesting in relation to the state of society
in his own time.

Henry the Minstrel, usually called Blind Harry,
composed the metrical " Life of Wallace " in the later
part of the fifteenth century. He earned his living by
travelling through the country and reciting his rhymes
to the people. His " Life of Wallace " has hardly any
historical value. The materials which he used in its
composition were the traditions, the stories, and the
ballads, then current among the people, touching
Wallace, which had been accumulating around his
name since his execution. It is thus an embodiment
of the notions and sentiments which the Scots en-

tertained about their greatest hero in the fifteenth
century. For this it is interesting and valuable.

James I. ranks among the poets of his age, and was
the author of a poem entitled "The King's Quair,"
which extends to 197 stanzas. It is animated, and
shows imaginative faculty, keen feeling, and marks of
real poetry. Robert Henryson, one of the most eminent of our early writers, was born in 1425, and died
toward the end of the century. He was the author of
various pieces of poetry which were much esteemed,
including thirteen moral fables in verse. His style is
easy and flowing, though it does not show great
passion or emotional power ; his realisation of the
beauties of external nature is very fine, and the associated objects are handled with rare skill.

The first Scotch University was a very simple
institution, and was originated by a few men who
formed an association in St. Andrews, under the
patronage of Bishop Wardlaw. They commenced to
deliver public lectures in 1410 ; and the Pope's Bull
sanctioning the establishment of the University
arrived in 1413. The event was celebrated with a
gladness and joy worthy of its significance. The
University of Glasgow was founded in 1451, but it
was poorly endowed. The University of Aberdeen
dates from 1494. A considerable part of the buildings of King's College, Aberdeen, belongs to the
beginning of the sixteenth century. The branches
usually taught in these schools were philosophy,
theology, and canon and civil law.

VIII.

PROGRESS OF THE REFORMATION IN SCOTLAND TO THE DEATH OF CARDINAL BEATON.

WE are now entering on the era of modern history, when influences which had been long working began to show themselves in unexpected forms. The languages of the chief nations of Europe were almost fully formed ; the various peoples were seeking unity and national independence ; and the printing press was ready to diffuse the new ideas as they appeared. The sixteenth century is a period of vast importance and interest in the annals of Europe, and in the development and civilisation of the human race. I shall narrate, as fully as the limits of this volume admit, the part which Scotland played in the revolutionary movement.

When Europe was on the eve of the Reformation, Scotland had lost her king on the disastrous field of Flodden. In October, 1513, his son, an infant, was crowned at Scone and his mother named Regent ; but this arrangement came to an end upon her marriage in the following year with the Earl of Angus. A party of the nobles were looking to the Duke of Albany as a likely personage to take the

reins of government.   He was a son of Alexander
Stuart, Duke of Albany, a brother of James III.,
and, after the infant king, was next heir to the throne.
He was an Admiral of France, whither his father had
fled, and where he himself lived in princely state.
Invited to the governorship of the kingdom, he
arrived in May, 1515, and was warmly welcomed by
the people, who hoped to enjoy an increase of peace
under his rule.   The task of restoring order among
the Scotch nobles was enormously difficult. Although
the new governor's talents were above the average of
his class, he laboured under the disadvantage of being
French in manner and habits, and of being un-
acquainted with the usages and feelings of the Scots.
He began his government with bold measures.
Offenders of the highest rank were seized, imprisoned,
and executed.   But these proceedings failed to produce the intended effect, and in a short time Albany
discovered the hopelessness of his task.   He repeatedly returned to France to be free of the turmoil;
and after a fluctuating sway of eight years, his regency
ended in 1524.

The Earl of Angus, who during Albany's regency
had been forced to flee the country, now returned to
push his claims to power.   With the concurrence of
the Earl of Arran and others, he became nominally
guardian of the king, and, in reality, his gaoler.   He
himself assumed the office of Chancellor of the
Kingdom, he made his uncle Treasurer, and they
compelled the king to sign everything which they
presented to him.   At last, in May, 1528, the king
escaped; and from that day to the end of his

reign, he pursued Angus and his accomplices with relentless severity.

Angus's estates were forfeited, and he was forced to flee to England. James appointed the Archbishop of Glasgow, Chancellor; the Abbot of Holyrood, Treasurer; and the Bishop of Dunkeld, Keeper of the Privy Seal. When the nobles were thus excluded from the government, they began to show a leaning toward the doctrines of the Reformation. Hating the clergy they became enraged at the ecclesiastical influence over the king; and as time passed and the prospects of the division of the Church lands approached, they grew firmer in their adherence to the principles of the Reformation.

But there were many causes of the Reformation, external and internal. The external causes were selfish and transient, and when the aims which stimulated their activity were gained, they ceased to operate. But the real religious sentiment was constant in its action and persistent in its manifestation in the face of fearful odds, till it attained its complete triumph in the recognition of religious freedom. The religious feeling, aspiration, and idea, were the real causes of the Reformation; and they involved social and political issues which were not foreseen by the politicians of the period. Political combinations in some quarters accelerated, and in others retarded, the religious movement; but all the political powers in the world could have neither accomplished nor prevented the final consummation of the Reformation. No external power can extinguish the internal operations of the human mind.

In 1525, Parliament prohibited the importation of Luther's books, and the propagation of his damnable opinions ; for the Scots had always adhered to the holy faith, and had never yet admitted any contrary opinion. Tyndale's version of the New Testament was brought into Scotland in 1526, and pretty freely circulated. In 1535, Parliament ordered all persons who had heretical books to deliver them to the authorities within forty days, under the penalty of imprisonment and confiscation.

The first Scotsman who suffered for the new opinions was Patrick Hamilton, the Abbot of Ferne. He had received the proscribed doctrines from the lips of Luther when sojourning in Germany. Having returned home in 1527, he began to teach what he had learned ; and early in the following year he was seized and imprisoned in the Castle of St. Andrews. He was tried for heresy, convicted, condemned, and burned on the 29th of February, 1528, before the College of St. Andrews. He left a short treatise in Latin, which contained a summary of his leading doctrines, and which was translated into English shortly after his death.

It was chiefly among the lower orders of the clergy that the new doctrines were embraced. The Friars were the preachers of the time, and here and there they would be found inveighing against the prevailing abuses of the priesthood. Friar William Airth had preached a sermon in Dundee, in which he touched on the lives of the bishops, and the evils associated with excommunication ; whereat the Bishop of Brechin's followers were greatly offended,

IACOBVS. V   REX. SCOTORVM,

JAMES V., KING OF SCOTLAND.

and they buffeted him as a heretic. The Friar undaunted, intimated that he would again preach in the parish church of St. Andrews; and on the appointed day the regents of the University and other persons of rank attended. He ascended the pulpit and gave out the text, " Verity is the strongest of all things." He referred to excommunication, and said that it should not be applied for every light cause, but only against open and incorrigible sinners. " But now," said he, " the avarice of priests and the ignorance of their office has caused it altogether to be utterly vilified; for the priest whose duty it is to pray for the people, stands up on Sunday and cries: ' One has tint a spurtle; there is a flail stolen beyond the burn; the good wife of the other side of the gate has tint a horn spoon; God's malison and mine I give to them that know of this gear and restore it not; '" so that the people only mocked such cursing.

The clergy held James V. faithful to the Church, and obtained his countenance to the persecution of the heretics. In 1534, after a truce of several years, proceedings were taken against a number of suspected persons, some of whom fled to England, and others renounced their opinions. Gourly, a priest, and Straiton, a layman, however, adhered to their heresy, and vindicated their faith; they were condemned in the presence of the king (who, it is said, would have granted them grace but for the intervention of the bishops), and were hanged and burned. Straiton's offence appears to have originated in his refusal to pay teinds to the prior of St. Andrews for fish caught

PALACE OF MARY OF GUISE, CASTLE HILL, EDINBURGH.

in his boat at sea. "If they would have teind thereof, which his servants won in the sea, it were but reason," he said, "they should come and receive it where he got the stock."

Henry VIII. wished James to throw off the authority of the Pope, and would gladly have seen the two countries brought together by a marriage with his daughter, the Princess Mary ; but his plans came to nothing. In 1537, James married Magdalen, daughter of the King of France. She died a few months after her arrival in Scotland ; and in the following year he married Mary, daughter of the Duke of Guise. The French alliance was thus secured, and the policy of the clergy confirmed.

The king pursued his policy of crushing the nobles. In 1541, Parliament passed an Act confirming the revocation of all grants of land, customs, borough rents, fishings, and gifts, which had been made during the king's minority. Another Act annexed to the Crown the Western, Orkney, and the Shetland Islands ; and also the lordships of Douglas, Bothwell, Preston, Tantallon, Crawford, Lindsay, Bonhill, Jedburgh Forest, Glammis, Liddesdale, Evandale. and the earldom of Angus, with all that belonged to it. Though these acts were within the limits of the constitution, they were overbold, as the Crown had not the power to enforce them. The nobles were nervously apprehensive, and their feelings soon became manifest.

While these events were passing at home, Henry VIII. was assuming a more dictatorial tone, and making demands which Scotland could not entertain.

In 1542, taking the occasion of James's failing to appear at an appointed conference at York, he proclaimed war. James mustered his army and marched southward, but tidings came that the English army had disbanded ; and the Scotch nobles then declined to follow their king. Their opportunity had come, and they resolved to mortify the man who had dared to encroach upon the rights of their class. The king was forced to disband the army. But he was extremely loth to abandon his intention of retaliating on Henry VIII., and shortly after it was agreed that a smaller force should make a raid across the border. This army mustered, advanced, and was approaching English ground when Oliver Sinclair, one of the king's favourites, began to read the commission which appointed himself to the chief command. The nobles present were enraged at this new encroachment upon their hereditary rights, a storm of indignation ensued, and all discipline was forgotten. Lord Dacre, the English leader, who was near at hand with three hundred cavalry, when he observed the confusion of the Scots, dashed in amongst them, and in an instant the Scottish army was scattered. A number of prisoners fell into the hands of the enemy, and among them nine nobles. This disaster is known in history as the panic of Solway Moss. When the tidings reached the king it broke his spirit ; he brooded over his disappointment and disgrace, gradually sank into a helpless state, and expired on the 14th of December, 1542.

The Crown then fell to an infant Mary Stuart, born in the palace of Linlithgow seven days before

THE EARL OF ARRAN.

the death of her father. She was destined to become
the most famous of the long line of Scottish
sovereigns. In her infancy and innocent childhood
she was an object of fierce contention. Her youth
and beauty, her talents and accomplishments, her
success and failure, the strength and weakness of her
character, her long captivity and tragic end—all
concurred to fill the story of her life with the most
absorbing interest.

James Hamilton, Earl of Arran, being next heir to
the throne, was elected regent. When Henry VIII.
heard of these events, he at once formed the idea
that he should have the infant queen for a wife to his
son, and it occurred to him that the banished Earl of
Angus, and the Scotch nobles taken at Solway Moss,
might be made useful agents for advancing his
scheme. He proposed to them accordingly that they
should exert themselves to place the infant queen in
his hands. To this Angus and several others consented, agreeing also to recognise Henry as Lord
Superior of Scotland, and to place the national castles
in his hands. The bond was drawn with great
formality, but Henry gained nothing by it.

The Regent Arran was not a man capable of
great resistance, and, left to himself, the temptations
which were held out to him, and which included the
marriage of his son to the Princess Elizabeth, would
have made him yield to the English king ; but the
strength of the national feeling against England
proved fatal to the scheme. So far had it gone that
treaties establishing an alliance between England and
Scotland and agreeing to a marriage between Prince

Edward and the young Queen of Scots had been concluded, subject only to ratification by the Scottish Parliament. The clergy, headed by Cardinal Beaton (who, on the death of his uncle in 1539, had become Archbishop of St. Andrews), were vehement against the scheme. There was much diplomatic wrangling, but the Cardinal triumphed. In December, 1543, Parliament repudiated the treaties, and, in the presence of the French ambassadors, renewed the ancient league with France.

Henry declared war, and avowed his intention of taking the infant queen by force. On the 11th of April, 1544, he issued instructions to the Earl of Hertford, which were marked with a ferocity of spirit unmatched in the annals of Europe. The earl was ordered to make an inroad into Scotland : " There to put all to fire and sword, to burn Edinburgh town, and to raze and deface it, when you have sacked it and gotten what you can of it, as there may remain for ever a perpetual memory of the vengeance of God lighted upon it for their falsehood and disloyalty. . . . Sack Holyrood House and as many towns and villages about Edinburgh as ye conveniently can. Sack Leith, and burn and subvert it, and all the rest, putting man, woman, and child to fire and sword without exception, when any resistance shall be made against you. And this done, pass over to the Fife land, and extend like extremities and destructions in all towns and villages whereunto ye may reach conveniently, not forgetting amongst all the rest, so to spoil and turn upside down the Cardinal's town of St. Andrews, as the upper stone may

HOLYROOD ABBEY.

be the nether, and not one stick stand by another, sparing no creature alive within the same, specially such as either in friendship or blood be allied to the Cardinal. The accomplishment of all this shall be most acceptable to the majesty and honour of the king." Hertford carried out his instructions, and led two expeditions into Scotland, one in May, 1544, and another in September. Towns and villages one after another were sacked and burned; and the monasteries of Melrose, Kelso, Holyrood, Jedburgh, Dryburgh, and other religious houses, were committed to the flames.

The instructions to Hertford reveal not only the bitterness of Henry's feeling towards the Scots, but also his especial detestation of Cardinal Beaton, who was the chief opponent of his policy. Numerous plots existed against the Cardinal's life. Henry encouraged them, and in effect offered a reward to any one who would rid him of his enemy. "And if the execution of this matter," wrote Sir Ralph Sadler to the Laird of Brunston, "doth rest only upon the reward of the king's majesty to such as shall be the executors of the same, I pray you advertise me what reward they do require, and if it be not unreasonable, because I have been in your country, for the Christian zeal that I bear to the common weal of the same, I will undertake it shall be paid immediately upon the act executed, though I do myself bear the charge of the same, which I would think well employed."

Meanwhile the persecution of those who had accepted the reformed doctrines, which were gradually spreading among the people, was undertaken with

CARDINAL BEATON.

increased vigour. The Cardinal held a court at
Perth in January, 1544, and many persons were
summoned and accused of heresy. A number of
them were banished ; but four men, James Hunter, a
flesher ; William Anderson, a maltman ; James Randl-
son, a skinner ; Robert Lamb, a burgess of Perth, and
his wife—were all condemned to death. The men
were hanged ; but the helpless woman, who had an
infant at her breast, was drowned. She gave her
infant to the attendants, her hands and feet were
bound, and she was thrown into a pool of water.

George Wishart, a popular reformed preacher,
returned to Scotland in the end of 1544. He was
supported by the Earls of Cassillis and Glencairn, the
Lairds of Brunston, Ormiston, and Calder, who were
deeply in league with Henry VIII., and were plotting
the murder of Cardinal Beaton ; but the evidence is
not conclusive that Wishart was implicated in the
plot. On the 16th of January, 1546, Wishart was
preaching in Haddington, accompanied by John
Knox. That same night he was apprehended at
Ormiston by the Earl of Bothwell, and conveyed
first to Edinburgh and shortly after to St. Andrews.
He was tried for heresy on the 28th of February,
condemned, and executed on the 11th of March.
The burning of this man aroused a deep feeling in
the popular mind, and many ventured to say that they
would not suffer the life of innocent men to be taken
away.

The Cardinal had endeavoured to strengthen his
position by the old custom of bonds with the nobles,
the Scotch faction opposed to his policy were dis-

HOUSE OF CARDINAL BEATON.

credited, and he was secure on the side of France. He passed through Fife, and attended the marriage of one of his natural daughters at Finhaven Castle. When enjoying himself, tidings came that Henry was preparing to invade Scotland, and he hurried home to put his castle in a defensive state. At that very time his enemies had matured their plot to murder him. He was living in his castle of St. Andrews, and had a number of men engaged in repairing it. Early on the morning of the 29th of May, 1546, Norman Lesly and other two men slipped into the castle. They were followed by James Melville and other three, who asked an interview with the Cardinal, and immediately after the Laird of Grange approached with eight armed men. This roused the suspicion of the porter at the gate, but he was instantly stabbed and cast into the ditch, and in a few minutes the party were within the walls of the castle. With surprising alacrity its defenders and the workmen on the ramparts were turned out, and all the gates shut and guarded. The unusual noise aroused the Cardinal from his bed, and he was ascending the stair when his enemies came upon him and ruthlessly murdered him. Meanwhile the alarm was raised in the city ; the common bell was rung, the citizens and the provost rushed in confusion to the castle, and called warmly and loudly for the Cardinal, but they were too late. Thus perished the ablest champion of Roman Catholicism in the kingdom.

IX.

REFORMATION MOVEMENT TO THE OVERTHOW OF
THE ROMAN CATHOLIC CHURCH IN SCOTLAND.

THE sixteen conspirators, joined by one hundred
and fifty others, succeeded for more than a year in
holding the castle of St. Andrews against the regent.
In April, 1547, John Knox joined the garrison, and
in May he assumed the functions of a preacher. A
congregation was formed in the city, to whom he
ministered, and a number of the citizens embraced
the reformed doctrines. After the siege had lasted
several months, the besiegers saw that they could not
take the place without investing it by sea as well
as by land, and, owing to the presence of the English
ships, this was impossible. In the end of June, 1547,
however, a number of French galleys appeared in
sight, and the attack was renewed from the seaward
side. This soon brought the defenders to submission.
The garrison surrendered to the French commander,
and were conveyed to France. Some of the chief
men were imprisoned ; the others, amongst whom
were John Knox and James Balfour and his two
brothers, were condemned to work as galley-slaves.

PORTRAIT AND AUTOGRAPH OF JOHN KNOX.

In 1549 Knox obtained his liberty, came to England, and preached in Berwick and Newcastle. He was appointed one of King Edward's chaplains in 1551. In March, 1554, he left England and passed to Geneva.

Henry VIII. died in January, 1547, while the castle of St. Andrews was still untaken, but his policy was continued. Lord Hertford, now Duke of Somerset, carried on the invasion of Scotland. The Scots were reduced to great extremities. Their crowning blow seemed to have come in a disastrous defeat at Pinkie in the autumn of 1547. Next year, however, a French army of seven thousand men arrived to assist them ; the young queen was sent to France, and thus one object of the war was removed. After many severe struggles, the French and the Scots drove the English out of the castles and recovered the southern part of the kingdom. Peace was at length concluded in 1550.

Though the pressure of external enemies was removed, the internal religious struggle proceeded. As the conflict of the old and the new religious views became clearer, and the shadow of the revolution was seen approaching, the Church and the Government acutely felt the gravity of the issues. In the ten years preceding 1560 four provincial councils of the Church were held in Scotland, at which were enacted one hundred and thirty-one canons, mostly directed against the immoral lives of the clergy, their ignorance, and the neglect of their duties. A strict and exhaustive search was ordered for heresy and heretical books, and especially poems and ballads. The

MARY OF GUISE, QUEEN REGENT.

party who wished to redress abuses without demo-
lishing the old Church prepared a catechism in the
vernacular for the use of the clergy, which is
characterised by moderate statement and by grace
of manner and of composition. It was intended as a
manual for the clergy to be read to the people. But
all the canons and the catechism were of no avail;
the accumulated corruptions of many generations had
resulted in a system of institutions incapable of reformation from within; the features of purity, the love
of truth and justice, had departed from their walls
and altars; the great ethical principles at the heart
of all true religion had waxed dim, and there were
no glowing rays to lighten up the darkness which
enveloped the Church.

In the end of the summer of 1550, Adam Wallace,
a layman from Ayrshire, a man of humble rank, was
accused of heresy. He was tried in Edinburgh before
the bishops, the regent, the Earl of Huntly, and others.
Amongst other things he was accused of having
assumed to preach without authority, and of reading the Scriptures. He denied having preached in
public, but admitted that he was in the habit of
reading the Bible, and that he had given such exhor-
tation as God had pleased to give him One of his
accusers said, "What, then, shall we leave to the
bishops and kirkmen to do, if every man shall be
a babbler upon the Bible?" Questions were put to
him touching the sacraments, prayer for the dead,
and other points. At last the Earl of Huntly asked
him what he thought of the mass. Wallace replied,
"That which is in greatest estimation before men

is abomination before God ; " whereat they all cried out, " Heresy ! heresy ! " He was condemned, and burned on the Castle Hill of Edinburgh.

Arran's regency was approaching its close. Through the vacillating character of his government he had fallen in public estimation, and the queen's mother was aspiring to the regency, and exerting all her influence to obtain it. Arran's party dwindling away, he resigned the regency in April, 1554, and Mary of Guise took his place. She was a woman of exceptional talents, and had acquired some knowledge of the character and habits of the Scots ; but she had many adverse influences and circumstances to contend against. Nevertheless, she ruled with remarkable moderation, and showed much sagacity and tact.

During the period of reaction and persecution in England under Mary and Philip of Spain, a number of Scotsmen who had formerly fled across the border returned home. Knox came back in September, 1555, and preached zealously against the mass. Amongst the hearers who approved his doctrines were the Prior of St. Andrews, afterwards known as the Regent Moray, the Earl of Argyle (then Lord Lorne), and other leading men. The Catholic clergy were alarmed, and Knox was summoned to appear at Edinburgh on the 15th of May, 1556. He resolved to appear, but when Erskine and other nobles who professed the new doctrines met in Edinburgh in force, the citation of Knox was abandoned. On the day that he should have appeared in court, he preached in Edinburgh to a larger audience than had ever listened to him. Soon after came to him a summons from the congregation in Geneva to repair to them as their pastor, and thither he proceeded accordingly.

Immediately after his departure the bishops again summoned him, and, on his failure to appear, had him burnt in effigy at the cross of Edinburgh. But

JOHN KNOX'S HOUSE.

the reformed doctrines continued to spread. William Harlaw, originally a tailor, a man of great zeal; John Willock, a native of Ayrshire, who in England had suffered imprisonment for the faith; John Douglas, a reformed friar; Paul Methven, originally a baker; and others, preached the new doctrines with great accept-

ance in various parts of the kingdom. A number of
the landed aristocracy came to an understanding as
adherents of the Reformation movement, for they
had cast their eyes on the property of the Church,
and this perhaps more than anything else stimulated
them to hasten on the revolution. In December,
1557, they joined in a bond known as the First
Covenant, to assist each other in advancing the
reformation of religion, in maintaining God's true
congregation, and renouncing the congregation of
Satan. Among those who subscribed this vigorously
worded document were the Earls of Argyle, Glencairn, and Morton, the Lord of Lorne, and John
Erskine, of Dun. The leaders of the movement
came to be known as "the Lords of the Congregation."

The feelings of the people began to appear in
many ways. Images were stolen and broken, and
monasteries were defaced. In Edinburgh the great
image of St. Giles was first drowned in the North
Loch, and afterwards burned. In some places the
images were hanged in mockery. At the same time
popular ballads and rhymes appeared, in which the
clergy and the abuses of Catholicism were sharply
and effectively assailed ; and all the efforts of the
government to suppress this class of writings utterly
failed. The rhymed, dramatic, and satirical writings
of Sir David Lindsay had a vast influence on the
people in relation to the Reformation—exposing the
abuses and corruptions of the existing system, and
completely destroying the national veneration so
long associated with it. Lindsay's composition and

phraseology is coarse and vulgar, but it was effective for its purpose. Indeed, his satire is too coarse for quotation; although his writings throw much light on the state of society.

In April, 1558, Walter Mill, an old man of over eighty years, a reformed priest, was apprehended and imprisoned in St. Andrews, and, being brought to trial, was convicted of heresy and burned. His execution tended to inflame the minds of the people and strengthen the position of the reform party, whose leaders gave warning that, unless such cruelties were stayed, they would be compelled to take up the sword for conscience' sake.

The queen regent for a time made a show of conciliation, but the French influence impelled her to open hostility. In 1559, after a meeting of the Ecclesiastical Council, a proclamation was issued prohibiting any person from preaching without authority from the bishops, and commanding the observance of the rites of the Catholic Church. Four of the chief preachers were cited to appear before the Justiciary Court at Stirling on the 10th of May, 1559, for convening the people, preaching erroneous doctrines, and inciting them to sedition. The Lords of the Congregation resolved to protect the preachers and mustered their feudal followers at Perth. John Knox had landed at Leith on the 2nd of May, and proceeded to join his brethren. An attempt was made to effect an arrangement with the regent, who promised to withdraw the citations, but she broke her word. The accused preachers were summoned, and, failing to appear, were proclaimed rebels.

This breach of faith so excited the people that only an occasion was needed to drive them to violence. On the 11th of May, after Knox had preached a vehement sermon against the mass in the parish church of Perth, a priest was so imprudent, or so contemptuous, as to uncover an altar in order to say mass. A youth exclaimed, at the top of his voice, "This is intolerable, that when God, by His Word, hath plainly damned idolatry, we shall stand and see it used in despite." The priest gave him a blow; he threw a stone at the priest which struck the tabernacle and broke one of the images. Instantly the multitude proceeded to cast stones and to tear down the altars and images and to destroy every vestige of the ornaments of the church. The mob proceeded to sack the monasteries of Grey Friars, Black Friars, and Charterhouse, and such was the destruction, that "within two days," says Knox, "the walls only did remain of all these great edifications." This example was followed in other places; and in an incredibly short time most of the religious houses in the kingdom were despoiled of their altars, images, and monuments.

The regent threatened the heavy punishment of all who had taken part in the outbreak at Perth; but she soon discovered that her power was not commensurate with her wishes. The Lords of the Congregation issued several manifestoes to the regent and to others in authority, all pervaded by a conviction of the truth and justice of their cause, and breathing a spirit of defiance and determination to carry out their views of reform. One of them, addressed " To the generation of Antichrist, the pestilent prelates and their shave-lings within Scotland," concluded thus: "We shall begin that same war that God commanded the Israelites to execute against the Canaanites; that is, contract of peace shall never be made, till ye desist from your open idolatry and cruel persecution of God's children. And this we signify unto you in the name of the eternal God, and of His Son, Jesus Christ, whose verity we profess, and evangel we will have preached, and holy sacraments rightly ministrate, so long as God will assist us to gainstand your idolatry. Take this for advertisement, and be not deceived."

The Lords of the Congregation were assembled in Perth with a considerable force under them. The regent's French troops advanced as far as Auch-terarder, when an arrangement was made through the influence of the Earl of Argyle and Stuart, the Prior of St. Andrews. The regent again broke faith, and the prior and Argyle then left her and joined the Congregation. The Lords, proceeding rapidly, invaded St. Andrews, and the primate fled. The regent's army approached, another treaty was made, and this also she failed to keep. She was expecting reinforce-ments from France to crush the heresy, and was desirous only of delay. Thus, failing to obtain peace, the Congregation took more vigorous measures. One division of their army entered Perth on the 25th of June; another under Argyle and the Prior of St. Andrews took possession of Edinburgh on the 29th, and the regent retired to Dunbar. They demolished the monasteries of the capital, and seized the coining irons of the Mint.

Tidings came that Henry II. of France was dead, and the husband of the Queen of Scots succeeded to the throne of that kingdom. This foreboded severer opposition to the Congregation, and they were soon in great distress. They left Edinburgh on the 26th of July, and retired to Stirling.

In August and September, a number of French troops disembarked at Leith, and began to fortify it. The Frenchmen soon made the defences so strong that the Lords of the Congregation could not hope to take the town. But they re-entered Edinburgh, and issued a proclamation deposing the regent from all authority. Skirmishing immediately began between them and the Frenchmen, and in these encounters the forces of the Congregation were generally defeated. Forced to retire from Edinburgh, they returned to Stirling. The reform party now resolved to make an urgent request to the English Government for assistance.

William Maitland of Lethington, who had joined the Congregation, proceeded to London with instructions to treat with Elizabeth and her Council, who were eager to detach Scotland from the French alliance. Knox had already been won over by Cecil, and Sir Ralph Sadler had reported that the French alliance was by no means so popular in Scotland as the English Council imagined. Much difficulty was occasioned by the fact that Elizabeth, the believer in divine right, felt herself treating with a body of men at war with their sovereign. But this was got over, and in January, 1560, the treaty of Berwick was concluded, whereby it was agreed to send English forces to expel the French from Scotland.

An English fleet, with six thousand men, appeared in the Firth of Forth. The united Scotch and English forces besieged Leith, but the French defensive works were strong and the attacks repeatedly repulsed. The garrison, however, began to feel sorely pressed, and provisions were failing; while the growing strength of the Protestants in France was rendering necessary the recall of the French troops. Negotiations were opened, and resulted in the treaty of Edinburgh on the 6th of July. It dealt with various matters touching the relations of France and England, some of which were never ratified. The articles more directly affecting the cause of the Congregation were mainly these :—That the French troops should depart (with the exception of one hundred and twenty men who were to hold the forts of Dunbar and Inchkeith); that the king and queen should not make peace or war except with the consent of the estates of the realm ; that neither the administration of civil and criminal justice, nor the high offices of the realm, should be deputed to aliens, and that churchmen should not hold the offices of treasurer and comptroller ; that a parliament should be assembled in August, and be as lawful as if it had been summoned by royal authority ; that there should be ordained "a law of oblivion," so that "all remembrance of bearing of armour and other things which have been done, shall be buried, earthed, and forgot," from the 6th of March, 1558. Peace was proclaimed on the 8th of July, and a few days after, the French and English troops departed.

The regent had retired into the castle of Edinburgh

on the approach of the English army. She was wearied and worn out with the responsibilities of her position, and died on the 10th of June, 1560.

Parliament assembled in the beginning of August, 1560, and there was an unusually large attendance. The leaders of the Reformation had prepared a petition to parliament setting forth their charges against the Church of Rome, and indicating the ways of redressing the existing enormities. It was a sweeping production and rather vehement in expression. One part of it referred to the patrimony of the Church, but Parliament waived this important question, and requested the reformers to lay before the House a summary of the doctrines which they proposed to establish. In four days they produced a Confession of Faith on the lines of the Confessions of the other Reformed Churches. On the 17th of August the Confession was read in parliament and adopted, three only of the nobles voting against it. The bishops and clergy did not oppose; and this fact, said the Earl Marischal, confirmed him in his belief of its truth. Parliament then passed an Act prohibiting, under penalties, the administration of the mass, and another which abolished the jurisdiction of the Pope in Scotland. These Acts, however, it should be remembered, did not receive the royal assent. The Scotch nobles had done their work, and laid the Church of their fathers in the dust; hereafter it will appear what was the depth of their religious feelings and convictions.

X.

REIGN OF QUEEN MARY.

In December, 1560, came news of the death of Francis II. This event was favourable to the leaders of the Reformation, for it limited, if it did not break, the ambitious schemes of the house of Guise. The work of reform proceeded in Scotland; and the nation looked for the early return of their queen.

After a series of interviews with James Stuart, Prior of St. Andrews, her natural brother, and with other personages, Mary resolved to return to the home of her ancestors. She embarked on the 14th of August, 1561, landed at Leith on the 19th, and all ranks of the people hastened to welcome her. It was a trying situation in which she found herself. The Scotch nobles, her natural counsellors, were a turbulent, jealous, and grasping class, while her religion was an offence to a great and increasing number of her subjects. Four days after her arrival, when the arrangements for the celebration of mass were made, such an outcry was raised that the chapel door had to be guarded, and order was with difficulty preserved. Next day it was proclaimed that till the assembly of

MARY QUEEN OF SCOTS.

the estates of the realm no one should take on hand to make any alteration or innovation of the state of religion which the queen had found established at her arrival, and, on the other hand, that no one should molest any of the queen's servants or attendants, in each case under pain of death. On the following Sunday Knox declaimed against the mass. That one mass of the previous week "was more fearful unto him," he said, "than if ten thousand armed enemies were landed in any part of the realm, of purpose to suppress the holy religion." Mary herself took him to task for stirring up her subjects against her, and for teaching sedition ; and even from Knox's own account of their interview, which is given in his history, one can see that she stood her ground with much spirit against his intolerant arguments.

As yet the Reformed Church could hardly be said to exist otherwise than on sufferance, for the head of the State was a Roman Catholic, and there was no provision for the Protestant ministers. Knox and his brethren were mistaken in supposing that the Lords of the Congregation would transfer the property of the old Church to the new one, and they so found when the proposals for disposing of the lands of the old establishment came before Parliament. At the General Assemby of 1561, when it was proposed that the queen should ratify the First Book of Discipline, which presented a worthy and admirable scheme for the application of the Church revenues, the question was asked, in jeering tones—"How many of those who have subscribed that book would be subject unto it?" They were sharply ordered to be content, as their proposals could not be entertained.

In December, 1561, an Act of the Privy Council proposed to appropriate a third of the revenue of all the benefices in the kingdom to the Crown. Thus the Catholic clergy were to retain the rents of their benefices, except this third which was to be applied to the purposes of the government, and to affording a reasonable provision for the Protestant ministry. The Reformed clergy were greatly displeased with the arrangement, and, in one of his sermons, Knox said: "Well, if the end of this order, pretended to be taken for the sustentation of the ministers, be happy, my judgment fails me; for I am assured that the Spirit of God is not the author of it; for, first, I see two parts freely given to the devil, and the third must be divided between God and the devil. Well, bear witness to me, that this day I say it, ere it be long, the devil shall have three parts of the third; and judge you then what God's portion shall be." Knox was near the truth, for by grants of lands, long leases, actual seizure, and other means, the nobles appropriated almost the whole of the property and revenue of the Roman Church.

The Earl of Huntly, the magnate of the north, did not change his religion; but the earldom of Moray was detached from his possession, and given to the Prior of St. Andrew's, James Stuart, then called Earl of Moray. The house of Huntly had ruled over the smaller chiefs in the Northern Highlands, and committed acts of great injustice. In

August, 1562, the queen and Moray marched northward ; and Huntly suspecting that a plot was forming
against him, sent his wife to Aberdeen to meet the
royal party and ascertain their purpose. She invited
the queen to the castle of Strathbogie, but Mary
declined, and advanced to Inverness. Some of the
clans who had been under Huntly, now that they
had the opportunity, deserted his standard and joined
the queen. The gates of the castle of Inverness were
closed against her, but the castle was soon taken, and
the garrison hanged. When the royal party returned
to Aberdeen, Huntly and his retainers followed them.
An engagement ensued, and Huntly was defeated
and slain. Thus Moray crippled the strongest family
to the north of the Tay. The queen proceeded by
Dundee, Perth, Stirling, and reached Edinburgh on
the 21st of November.

The Court stayed in Edinburgh through the winter.
The gaiety of the queen gave great offence to Knox,
who traced her excessive dancing to the progress of
the persecution in France ; for " he was assured," he
says, " that the queen had danced excessively till
after midnight, because she had received letters that
persecution was begun in France, and that her uncles
were beginning to stir their tails and to trouble the
whole realm of France "—whereupon he preached a
sermon on the vices of princes. When Mary heard
of this sermon she sent for Knox ; and he was
accused of speaking irreverently, and making the
queen an object of hatred and contempt among her
people. In self-defence, he rehearsed from memory
what he had said in the pulpit, thus : " For princes

will not understand ; they will not be learned
as God commands them. But God's law they
despise, His statutes and holy ordinances they will
not understand ; for in fiddling and flinging they are
more exercised than in reading or hearing God's
most blessed Word ; and fiddlers and flatterers (which
commonly corrupt the youth) are more precious in
their eyes than men of wisdom and gravity. . . .
And of dancing, Madam, I do not utterly damn it,
provided two vices be avoided—the former that the
principal vocation of those that use that exercise be
not neglected for the pleasure of dancing ; and,
second, that they dance not, as the Philistines their
fathers, for the pleasure that they take in the displeasure of God's people." The queen said, "Your
words are sharp enough as ye have spoken them, but
yet they were told to me in another manner. I know
that my uncles and ye are not of one religion, and
therefore I cannot blame you, albeit you have no
good opinion of them."

The flow of events seemed likely to engulf the
Reformed party in a sea of trouble. The queen
was preparing for her marriage with the son of the
Earl of Lennox. After twenty years' banishment,
the earl arrived in Edinburgh on the 23rd of September, 1564, and in December his titles and estates
were restored. Henry, Lord Darnley, his eldest son,
came to Edinburgh on the 12th of February, 1565.
To him, failing direct heirs of Elizabeth and Mary,
would fall the succession to both the English and the
Scottish Crowns. He was young and handsome, but
vain and ambitious, and devoid of ability and moral

character; and he had not been many weeks in Scotland before he had made enemies. The Earl of Moray, who had acted as head of the government since the queen's return from France, was strongly opposed to the marriage; and his party formed an aversion to Darnley. As Darnley was a Roman Catholic, this intensified the difficulties of the nation. Moray concerted measures to prevent the queen's marriage; but a special meeting of the nobles and officers of State was held at Stirling in May, and

CIPHER OF LORD DARNLEY AND QUEEN MARY.

Mary announced to them her intention to marry Darnley.

The General Assembly, in June, 1565, passed certain resolutions for the purpose of being enacted by Parliament and ratified by the queen. Amongst other things, they demanded that the mass, with all papistical idolatry and papal jurisdiction, should be suppressed and abolished throughout the realm, not only in the subjects, but also in the queen's own person. Mary replied that she was not yet persuaded in the Protestant religion, nor that there was any impiety in the mass ; that, to deal plainly with her subjects, she neither would nor might leave the religion wherein she had been nourished and brought up ; that she had not in the past, and did not intend thereafter to press the conscience of any, and that they on their part should not press her conscience.

Moray and his party met at Stirling on the 15th of July, to consult on the project of rebellion ; but the same day the queen issued a proclamation calling on all loyal subjects to prepare themselves to attend her for fourteen days in the field. A general muster of the Crown vassals was ordered on the 22nd of July. Offers were made to Moray to appear before the council and obtain satisfaction. The intended marriage was proclaimed ; and on the 29th of July Mary and Darnley were joined in wedlock, amid the rejoicing of the people at Holyrood.

Moray and his associates—the Duke of Chatelherault, the Earls of Argyle, Glencairn, Rothes, and other barons—mustered a thousand of their followers, and they were proclaimed rebels. After trying various movements, they were unable to face the royal army in the field. They retired to Dumfries, and at last disbanded, and fled to England.

The queen had triumphed. Many of the Protestants thought that the Reformation would be extinguished in Scotland. There were many plots among the Roman Catholic States of Europe for the total overthrow of all heresy. Spain was deeply interested in the recovery of Britain to the Holy See, but the stream of events swept away this dream.

Mary's marriage was extremely unhappy. Her husband was a vain and vicious man ; and their domestic quarrels soon became notorious. The queen had several foreigners in her service, and one named Riccio acted as her foreign secretary ; he enjoyed her confidence, and she occasionally consulted him on important matters. But Darnley imagined that Riccio was his enemy, that he had prevented the queen from granting him the Crown matrimonial—from one silly thought to another he ran to the conclusion that Riccio had frustrated his object. The Scotch nobles quickly saw Darnley's weakness. Seeking a way to restore the rebel lords, they seized hold of him as their tool, and on Riccio as their victim.

Parliament was summoned to meet at Edinburgh on the 4th of March, 1566, and it was intended to confiscate the estates of the rebel lords ; but they had many friends in Scotland and even in Parliament. The Scotch nobles were never deficient in devising plots for the overthrow of their enemies and the attainment of their own ends. Morton, the Chancellor of the kingdom, Lord Lindsay, Lord Ruthven, and others, entered into a bond with Darnley for the murder of Riccio, and to secure the restoration of the rebel lords—Moray and his associates. Darnley was the mere plaything of the nobles, for they had no intention of elevating him to the throne ; their chief aim was to prevent the proceedings of Parliament, and thus preserve intact the estates of the rebel lords.

The plot was well matured, and everything prepared for its realisation. On the 7th of March

DOORWAY IN WHICH RICCIO WAS MURDERED.

Parliament was opened by the queen in person, but Darnley, instead of accompanying her, rode off to Leith. The evening of the 9th of March was fixed for the consummation of the dismal deed. Morton, with one hundred and sixty armed men, took possession of the inner court of the palace and guarded the gates ; a party of these were placed in the royal audience chamber on the ground floor. Thence Darnley ascended to the queen's apartments, and Lord Ruthven accompanied him. They found their victim sitting with his cap on his head in her Majesty's presence ; some parley and sharp talk passed between the queen and Ruthven ; but shortly more of the conspirators rushed in, and instantly the tables and chairs were overturned, and David Riccio was seized and dragged to an outer room, and there stabbed to death. A guard was placed over the queen ; but in spite of this several persons escaped and warned the citizens of Edinburgh. The alarm bell was rung, the citizens rushed to the palace and demanded the instant deliverance of the queen, but she was not permitted to speak to them. Darnley appeared and assured the citizens that she was safe, and commanded them to retire. Ruthven and Darnley prepared two proclamations to be issued next day in the name of the king—the one ordered the citizens to keep order on the streets, the other dissolved Parliament, and commanded all the members to leave the capital, except those whom the king might request to remain. Lord Ruthven placed men to watch the gates, but the Earls of Huntly and Bothwell escaped.

THE REGENT MORTON.

The following day the rebel lords arrived seized
Edinburgh and frustrated the proceedings of Parliament. Mary soon disengaged her husband from the
nobles who had murdered her favourite servant;
and five days after the tragedy they slipped out at
midnight and rode to Seton House, and thence to
Dunbar. The rebellious nobles rose in the morning
and found that they had been outwitted, and were in
imminent danger. An army quickly rallied round
the queen, and she advanced on Edinburgh. The
rebel nobles were not prepared to meet her, and they
dispersed : Morton and Ruthven fled to England,
others fled to the Highlands, and some of them
retired to their own estates. After a short time the
queen pardoned Moray and some of his associates ;
but she declined to pardon those directly implicated
in the murder of Riccio. Still only two subordinate persons were executed in connection with this
crime.

Mary retired into the castle of Edinburgh, and on
the 19th of June, 1566, James VI. of Scotland and
I. of England was born. After this event, the queen
listened to suggestions for reconciliation with the
rebellious nobles. Though Huntly and Bothwell
were at the head of the Government, Moray, Argyle,
Glencairn, and others, were readmitted to a share in
the administration. Bothwell had rapidly risen to a
high position.

A series of stirring events and plots issuing in
tragedy, and the final disaster of the queen, occurred
in rapid succession. The Scotch aristocracy had long
pursued a line of policy which directly depressed the

authority of the Crown, and they would not let an
opportunity slip without turning it to their own
advantage.

A plot for the murder of Darnley was concocted.
According to custom a bond was drawn by Sir James
Balfour, a lawyer and a friend of Bothwell ; the bond
declared that Darnley " was a young fool and tyrant,
and unworthy to rule over them." Therefore they
bound themselves to remove him by some means or
other, and all agreed to stand true to each other in
this deadly enterprise. The bond was signed by the
Earls of Huntly, Argyle, Morton, and others who
joined the conspiracy. Their victim had become
sick, and he was visited by the queen at Glasgow,
whence he was conveyed to Edinburgh on the last
day of January, 1567. He was put into a house
close to the city wall, called " Kirk of Field." The
queen was very attentive to him, and for several
nights before his murder she slept in a room below
him.

At last everything seemed to have been prepared,
and the evening of Sunday, the 9th of February, was
fixed for the murder. In the Court everything was
going on in the most joyful fashion ; that evening
Moray left to join his wife at St. Andrews ; and the
same night a marriage was to be celebrated between
two of the queen's servants. Meanwhile Bothwell
and his accomplices were intently engaged in making
the preparations for their horrible deed. They had
resolved to blow up the house by gunpowder, and
after dark they placed a large quantity of it in the
room below the king, and Bothwell superintended

the operations. At ten o'clock in the evening the queen passed from Holyrood and joined her husband. There was some agreeable conversation between them ; and then Mary recollected that she had promised to attend the ball to be held that night in honour of the marriage of her two servants. She bade Darnley farewell, and departed with Bothwell and Huntly. Apparently only two of the conspirators remained about the king's house, and at the last moment some hitch seems to have occurred. Darnley and his servant had discovered their danger and attempted to escape, but were caught in the garden and strangled to death. Bothwell, with a company of his followers, returned from Holyrood about midnight and joined the other two conspirators, who had already lighted the train. The explosion shook the earth for miles around, and roused the citizens of Edinburgh ; and Bothwell ran to his apartment in the palace and immediately went to bed, only to be awakened as if from slumber half an hour after, by a message informing him of the tragedy, and then, like an honest and innocent man, he shouted, " Treason ! Treason ! " With the Earl of Huntly he called on the queen to tell her what had happened.

It was well known that Bothwell was the chief actor in the crime, but at the time no one would have been safe to accuse him ; and many of the nobles were deeply implicated in the conspiracy. The murder caused great excitement ; and printed bills were fixed on the door of the Parliament house naming Bothwell, Balfour, and others as the guilty parties. Darnley's remains were privately interred in the chapel of Holyrood ; and the day after the queen, with Huntly, Argyle, Bothwell, and the Archbishop of St. Andrews, removed to Seton House. Bothwell with a party of armed men on horseback, came from Seton House to Edinburgh, paraded the streets, and with hideous oaths and furious gestures loudly declared "that if he knew who were the authors of the bills, he would wash his hands in their blood."

Rumours arose that the queen would marry Bothwell. The Earl of Lennox naturally and properly insisted that the parties who had murdered his son should be brought to trial. At last Lennox was summoned to attend the trial of Bothwell as a party to the action. The Council ordered Bothwell and others to be tried by jury on the 12th of April, 1567. On the appointed day Bothwell had three thousand of his armed retainers on the streets of Edinburgh. The Court met ; he appeared and certain forms of law were gone through, but no witnesses appeared against him, and he was acquitted. He then published a challenge offering single combat to any one, noble or common, rich or poor, who dared to affirm that he was guilty of the murder of Darnley. As no one responded to his challenge, he might aver that he had satisfied the law and the ancient custom of his country.

Two days after his trial Parliament met, and he bore the crown and sceptre before the queen when she rode to the Parliament house. A number of Acts were passed, chiefly relating to grants of lands.

Bothwell got a grant of lands which included the castle of Dunbar.

The day after Parliament rose, Bothwell invited the nobility to a banquet at an hotel in Edinburgh, and a large party attended. After the red wine had been freely quaffed, which made their hearts warm and their faces shine, he placed before them a bond and kindly requested them to sign it. The bond stated that Bothwell's private enemies had malignantly slandered and accused him of complicity in the heinous murder of the late king ; but that he was now acquitted, and had also, according to ancient custom, offered to prove his innocence by single combat : it referred to the nobleness of his house and the honourable service rendered by his predecessors to the Crown, and especially by himself to her Majesty the Queen, "in the defence of her realm against the enemies thereof ; " and considering that it was ruinous to the kingdom for the queen to remain a widow, it went on to recommend Bothwell as the most suitable match she could obtain among her own subjects. All those who signed the bond undertook upon their honour " to promote and set forward the marriage to be solemnised between her highness and the said noble lord, with our votes, counsel, and assistance, in word and in deed, to the utmost of our power, at such time as it should please her Majesty to fix, and as soon as the law shall allow it to be done." All the nobles present signed this bond, save the Earl of Eglinton, who slipped away.

On the 21st of April, the queen visited her son in

QUEEN MARY'S ROOM, CRAIGMILLAR CASTLE.

Stirling Castle, and stayed two days. When returning to Edinburgh she was met by Bothwell, at the
head of a party of his retainers, and conveyed to the
castle of Dunbar. He shortly after conducted the
queen to the castle of Edinburgh, and preparations for
the marriage were rapidly pushed forward. Bothwell
obtained a divorce from his own wife on the 7th of
May, 1567 ; the banns of marriage between him and
the queen were proclaimed on the 12th of May ;
and, three days after, their marriage was celebrated in
the palace of Holyrood.

But, unfortunately, the current of events soon
ruffled the happiness of the newly-wedded pair.
Troubles gathered fast around the unhappy queen.
Bothwell and she left Edinburgh on the 7th of June,
and passed to Borthwick Castle, about ten miles
south of the capital. Morton and Lord Home with
an army appeared before it, and Mary and Bothwell
escaped with difficulty to the castle of Dunbar.
They were now greatly alarmed, and commanded the
Crown vassals of the district to muster immediately.
The opposing party—the confederate nobles—seized
Edinburgh, arranged with James Balfour, the governor of the castle, and at once assumed all the
functions of government. Mary and Bothwell had
mustered between two and three thousand men, and
advanced upon Edinburgh. The confederate nobles
determined to meet them ; and the two armies
approached each other near Musselburgh. After a
day's manœuvring and treating, during which Bothwell challenged any of his accusers to single combat,
two men of the second rank and several of the

first stepped forward and offered to fight him single-
handed, but the queen would not permit the combat.
At last Mary surrendered to the nobles, and Bothwell
was allowed to ride off in the direction of Dunbar.
The queen was taken to Edinburgh on the 15th of
June, and on the 17th she was conveyed a captive to
Lochleven.

The confederate nobles rapidly developed their

MUSSELBURGH BRIDGE.

scheme in accordance with their traditions, which
simply consisted in taking the powers and rights of
the Crown into their own hands.   Accordingly they
resolved to dethrone the queen, place the crown on
her infant son, and appoint the Earl of Moray regent.
In the island of Lochleven on the 23rd of June,
they presented two documents to Mary, which they

requested her to sign ; the one was a renunciation of her crown, and the other the appointment of Moray to the regency. Under severe pressure Mary yielded to these terms, and Parliament ratified them. The next step, according to custom, was to place the infant upon the throne, and James VI., a baby of thirteen months old, was solemnly crowned in the parish church of Stirling on the 29th of July, 1567. The two deeds which Mary signed were publicly read ;

LOCH LEVEN AND CASTLE.

the Earl of Morton took the coronation oath for the Prince and Steward of Scotland ; then the Bishop of Caithness anointed him " the most excellent Prince and King of this realm." John Knox concluded the proceedings by a sermon, which he delivered in his most vigorous style. The following day the king's authority was proclaimed ; and the reign of Queen Mary, in fact and in law, ceased.

XI.

CONFLICT OF THE NATION TO THE UNION OF THE CROWNS.

THUS far the revolutionary movement had awakened and stirred society ; but as yet the nation was much divided. The Earls of Morton, Athole, Mar, Glencairn, Lord Lindsay, Lord Home, and others, with Moray as their leader, were supported by the Reformed clergy ; on the other hand, a section of the Protestant nobles stood aloof and disapproved of the treatment of the queen, while the Roman Catholic party were constantly active and looking for their opportunity. On all sides were the elements of conflict.

On the 22nd of August, 1567, Moray assumed his office, took the oath required by the constitution, and was proclaimed regent. The seals were called in and broken, and new ones made with a legend appropriate to James VI. Moray struggled hard to restore order and administer justice, and he soon obtained possession of the chief castles of the kingdom. Parliament met at Edinburgh in December, "to treat on the affairs tending to the glory of God, establishing of the king's authority, and good and necessary laws in the kingdom." The Acts passed in 1560, which had never received the royal assent, were confirmed, and the Confession of Faith was inserted in the parliamentary record. The revolution which had substituted Protestantism for Catholicism might be regarded as assured, though much still remained to be settled. The General Assembly appointed a committee of its members to consult with Parliament and the Government at all times touching the affairs of the Church. But the queen's party were exceedingly active, and it was evident that disaffection existed.

Early in May, 1568, Mary escaped from Lochleven, and proceeded to Hamilton. Her chief adherents were, besides the Hamiltons, Argyle, Huntly, Rothes, Seton, Cassillis, Harris, Livingston, Fleming, and Claud Hamilton ; and within a few days the force at their command numbered six thousand men. The regent was in Glasgow when tidings of the queen's escape reached him. He determined at once to meet the danger, ordered a muster of all the Crown vassals, and, marching from Glasgow, took up a position at Langside. On the 13th of May the queen's followers gave him battle, but he completely defeated them, and Mary fled toward the border. In an unhappy hour she resolved to throw herself upon the protection of the Queen of England. After suffering twenty years' imprisonment in England, she was beheaded on the 8th of February, 1587.

The regent continued his efforts to maintain order, but it was difficult, as he had a host of enemies, and his position tended to multiply them. Sir William

Kirkaldy of Grange, governor of Edinburgh Castle, and Maitland of Lethington, joined the queen's party ; the other centres of her supporters were the Hamiltons and Argyle in the west, some of the border clans in the south, and Huntly in the north. Thus beset, the regent was hard pressed, but he struggled on bravely. As the castle of Edinburgh was in the hands of his enemies, he marched for Stirling early in 1570; and when returning through Linlithgow on the 23rd of January, he was shot by Hamilton of Bothwellhaugh, and expired in a few hours. The assassin escaped on a fleet horse and rode to Hamilton Castle. Moray's death was greatly bewailed by the Reformed clergy and many of the people, who looked on him as the arm of their safety.

For several years the factions of the king and queen kept the kingdom in an incessant turmoil. In July, 1570, the Earl of Lennox, the king's grandfather, was elected regent, and assumed the government. Both parties issued proclamations and counter manifestoes ; and there was much skirmishing about Edinburgh. Knox fought with all the force and vehemence of his nature on the king's side. But in October he sustained a shock of apoplexy which impaired his speech. The General Assembly instructed all the ministers to pray for the king and the submission of the people to his authority. Parliament met at Stirling in August, 1571 ; at the same time the queen's party held their parliament in Edinburgh. In the latter, sentences of forfeiture were passed against the Earl of Morton and other chiefs of the king's party ; in the former, Acts were passed in favour of Morton and Lord Lindsay, as a reward for their resistance to the enemies of the king, and also in favour of those who had taken the castle of Dumbarton. When they were thus engaged, a company of the queen's adherents, under the Earl of Huntly and Lord Hamilton, marched from Edinburgh on Stirling, surprised them, and slew the Regent Lennox on the 4th of September. The Earl of Mar was chosen regent, but he died on the 28th of October, 1572.

The Earl of Morton, who had been the leading spirit of the king's party since the death of Moray, was then elected regent. He had been implicated in all the great plots of the last twenty years; he was an ambitious and crafty man, but able, brave, and determined like all his ancestors of the Douglas tribe: Morton courted the friendship of the English Government; and in the spring of 1573 he concluded an arrangement by which one thousand five hundred English troops and a train of artillery entered Scotland, and assisted in the reduction of the castle of Edinburgh. The queen's party in the country were broken, and most of the leaders had submitted to the regent. The castle of Edinburgh surrendered in the end of May. The common soldiers of the garrison were dismissed; but the governor, Kirkaldy of Grange, and his brother, were hanged at the cross of Edinburgh. Maitland of Lethington, who had in his time hatched so many plots, and attempted to play so many parts, at last saved himself from the scaffold by committing suicide. After this Mary's party in Scotland were completely subdued.

Knox had been in feeble health for some time, but his mind continued vigorous to the last. On Sunday, the 9th of November, 1572, he officiated at the induction of James Lawson as his colleague and successor in Edinburgh. His voice was weak, and this was the last time that he appeared in public. On the 11th he was seized with a severe cough; but he continued cheerful, and was surrounded by his family, and visited by many friends. He died on the 24th of November, in the sixty-seventh year of his age, and

GRAVE OF JOHN KNOX.

on the 26th his remains were interred in the church-yard of St. Giles. His character is manifested in his work. In co-operation with his contemporaries, he brought blessings to the people of Scotland which they have never forgotten. Although he was strong in assertion and firm in his own convictions, he was even stronger in denial and negation, as he swept off the accumulated mass of legends, traditions, and ceremonies which had enslaved the mind, and

obscured the glory, the purity, and the truth of
Christianity.

The Reformed clergy devoted much of their energy
to the improvement of the polity of the Church,
and the planting and organisation of congregations
throughout the kingdom. Under the able leader-
ship of Andrew Melville they formed and adopted
the presbyterian form of polity which obtained a very
strong hold of the national mind, although it was
persistently opposed by the Crown and the Government. Morton favoured the episcopal form of polity,
but he was never popular, and early in 1578 he resigned the regency. The government was committed
to a council of twelve members, mostly· nobles, and
the young king then in his twelfth year. Although
Morton had resigned, he was still feared, and
therefore his enemies were plotting his utter ruin.

In 1579 Eme Stuart, a cousin of the king, arrived
from France, and soon became a special favourite of
the king. The two were constantly together ; whatever interested the one was sure to interest the other,
and the result was that Eme speedily rose to greatness.
He was first created an earl, and shortly after Duke
of Lennox, and was appointed High Chamberlain
and governor of the castle of Dumbarton. Captain
James Stuart, another of the king's favourites, was
elevated to the rank of Earl of Arran in 1581. But
the two upstarts were insecure as long as Morton
was at liberty, and therefore the Duke of Lennox
accused him of complicity in the murder of Darnley,
the king's father. The fallen regent was seized and
imprisoned in the castle of Edinburgh. He was

tried on the 1st of June, 1581, and, on his own confession that he was privy to the plot for the murder of Darnley, he was condemned, and beheaded on the 2nd of June.

Lennox and Arran were now supreme in the government. As usual a party of the nobles entered into a bond to crush them, take the king into their own hands, and rule the kingdom themselves. The young king was very fond of sport, and he was invited to Ruthven Castle, in the vicinity of Perth, to enjoy his favourite amusement. The Earl of Ruthven warmly welcomed him; but when the king arose in the morning he was much alarmed by the number of armed men around the castle, and soon discovered that he was a prisoner. The Earl of Arran was seized and imprisoned, and the Duke of Lennox ordered to leave the kingdom. This plot is known in history as " The Raid of Ruthven."

In a few days the king was removed to Stirling, and in October, 1582, he was conveyed to Holyrood Palace. Parliament was assembled, and an Act of indemnity to the chief actors in the plot was passed. Having thus, according to custom, passed a vote of thanks to themselves, they proclaimed that under the providence of God they were moved to attempt the reform of many abuses which threatened to subvert the existing religion and the majesty of the Crown of the kingdom. The clergy and the General Assembly approved of these proceedings, and explained their object to the people.

But the king escaped in June, 1583, and the power of the Ruthven party was broken. Most of the nobles implicated fled to England. The Earl of Gowrie was seized, tried for treason, condemned, and beheaded at Stirling in May, 1584. Meanwhile the clergy were intensely alarmed, as they had approved of the Ruthven enterprise. Andrew Melville, the leader of the Reformed clergy, was summoned before the Privy Council touching a sermon which he had preached. He explained the sermon, but the Council resolved to proceed with his trial ; he then protested, and declined to answer, on the ground that the case in the first instance ought to be tried by the presbytery. His protest greatly irritated and touched the vanity of the king, and on the second day of the trial Melville told him and his council that they had assumed too much in attempting to control the servants of God, and said that the laws of the kingdom were perverted in his case. The court ordered him to be imprisoned in the Castle of Blackness within ten hours ; but Melville preferred to choose his own place of imprisonment, and immediately fled to Berwick.

The contest between the Crown and the clergy had reached a crisis. Archbishop Adamson, in concert with the king, was concocting a scheme for the reintroduction of Episcopacy. He drew up a series of articles which recognised in emphatic terms that the king was the head of the Church, and that therefore it was his prerogative to appoint the order of her polity. On the other hand, it was pointed out that presbyteries in which laymen associated with the clergy were a continual source of sedition. These ideas were instilled into the king's mind at this impressible period of his life, and throughout his reign he never ceased to enforce them to the utmost of his power.

In the beginning of May, 1584, several of the preachers fled to Berwick and joined Melville, and the banished nobles. On the 19th of May, Parliament met, and passed a series of Acts which placed in the king's hands unprecedented powers. One Act affirmed his supreme authority in all matters civil and religious ; another enacted that to speak against any of the proceedings of Parliament should be accounted treason ; and all the Acts and decisions of the Church Courts, if unsanctioned by Parliament, were to be held unlawful. All meetings to consult on any matter without the king's special license were unlawful. All comment on the proceedings of the king and Council was prohibited under severe penalties. And that these powers, which by the gift of heaven belonged to his Majesty and to all his successors on the throne, should continue unimpaired, it was necessary to condemn Buchanan's " History of Scotland " and his " De Jure Regni apud Scotos," and, therefore, all who possessed copies of these books were ordered to deliver them to the royal officers within forty days, " that they may be purified of the extraordinary matters which they contain."

When the Acts were proclaimed, three of the ministers—Lawson, Pont, and Balcanquhal—protested against them as injurious to the liberties of the Church. Soon after more than twenty of the ministers fled to England. The king and his party, having obtained an ample recognition of their supreme power, resolved to crush the rebellious preachers and nobles. Parliament re-assembled in August. A process of treason was passed against the banished nobles, and their lands were forfeited. An Act was passed commanding all clergymen, masters of colleges and of schools, to sign and humbly promise to obey the Acts of the last Parliament ; and to show their submissive spirit, they were ordered to obey the bishops appointed to rule over them. All the ministers between Stirling and Berwick were summoned to appear at Edinburgh on the 16th of November, 1584, and attest their submission to the king. Under the threat of losing their stipends, a majority of them yielded ; but it soon appeared that they were not subdued.

Lord Maxwell had been for many generations the leading noble in Dumfries and its neighbourhood ; but the king had ventured to encroach upon his local supremacy in the election of a provost. Maxwell was therefore at war with the king, and mustered a thousand men ; and the banished nobles saw their opportunity and joined him. In November, 1585, they returned and collected their adherents, met Maxwell at Selkirk, and thence with an army of eight thousand men marched on Stirling. The king and Arran were in Stirling when the rebels approached. Arran fled to the Highlands, and the king had no alternative but to receive the proffered homage of his rebellious nobles and pardon them. Most of the exiled ministers returned with the nobles, and resumed their functions. After a severe struggle with the Crown, the Presbyterian party prevailed.

The General Assembly in May, 1592, resolved to petition Parliament to pass an Act recognising the polity and liberties of the Church. Parliament assembled at Edinburgh in June, and an Act was passed which confirmed all the liberties granted to the Church by the regents and the king. It recognised and sanctioned the General Assemblies, synods, presbyteries, and sessions of the Church. The Act of 1584, touching the royal supremacy, and the Act relating to the bishops were expressly repealed. Although this Act is incomplete, it has always been regarded by the Presbyterian body as an important step in the national reformation.

Still there were rumours of plots, and designs of the Jesuits ; and the clergy were annoyed at the lenity of the king to the Catholic nobles of Huntly, Errol, and Angus. They were constantly on the outlook for their enemies. In February, 1593, the king made a demonstration against the Catholic earls, and they retired to Caithness. But the Reformed clergy insisted on the complete submission of the Catholics. The Catholic earls thus driven to extremities rebelled, and the Earl of Argyle was commissioned to muster his vassals and march against them. The undisciplined army under him was attacked by the Earls of Huntly and Errol in Glenlivet on the 13th of October, 1594, and after a severe engagement, he was completely defeated, and his followers fled in confusion. The king had advanced to Dundee when tidings of Argyle's defeat reached him, and he proceeded with his army to Aberdeen, where several of the local chiefs joined him. Andrew Melville and a number of other popular preachers accompanied the army, which advanced into the centre of the enemy's territory. Huntly was unable to face the royal army, and fled to Caithness. His stronghold, the castle of Strathbogie, was dismantled; the castle of Slaines, the seat of the Earl of Errol, and other mansions, were also defaced. On returning to Aberdeen, the king caused a number of Huntly's followers to be executed, and then proclaimed pardon to those who had been at the battle of Glenlivet, if they paid the fines imposed by the Council. After making some arrangements for securing peace in the district, the army was disbanded, and the king returned to Stirling on the 14th of November. The Catholic earls were reduced to despair, and left Scotland in March, 1595.

But the clergy never relaxed their efforts, fearing that the Catholic nobles would return. They did return in the summer of 1596, and the king seemed inclined to restore them. The body of the clergy were opposed to this, and selected a committee of sixteen of their own number to sit in Edinburgh, and act in concert with the ministers of the capital. The king tried to convince the clergy of the justice of his proposal to restore the Catholic earls, but utterly failed. Mr. Black, one of the ministers of St. Andrews, delivered a vehement sermon in which he assailed the king, the court of session, and the nobles, in the most outspoken style. He was immediately summoned before the Privy Council, and appeared, but declined its jurisdiction. The king was enraged at the preacher's denial of his supremacy, and commanded the committee of the Church to depart from Edinburgh, and announced that the ministers should sign a bond to obey the king and the Privy Council before they received their stipends. His flatterers keeping him on the line of thought and the mode of feeling to which he had always been inclined, he next commanded twenty-six of the most ardent Protestants in Edinburgh to depart within six hours. The excitement in the capital then became extreme. On the 17th of December, a rumour spread that Huntly had been at the palace of Holyrood. Balcanquhal was ascending the pulpit when this story was told to him, and unaware of its falsehood, he commented on it in his sermon, and raised the feeling of the congregation. At the close of his sermon, he called on the barons present not to disgrace their names and their ancestors, but to meet the ministers immediately in the Little Church. A crowd had collected, and the preacher addressed them on the danger to which the Church was exposed by the return of the Catholic earls.

A deputation waited on the king, who was in the council chamber with the lords, and informed him that they were sent by the barons convened in the Little Church, to lay before his Majesty the dangers which threatened religion. "What danger see you," said the king, "and who dares to assemble against my proclamation?" Lord Lindsay replied, "We dare do more than that, and will not suffer religion to be overthrown." The clamour increased and a number of the people rushed into the room;

the king in great alarm started to his feet, and
without giving any answer, ran down the stairs and
ordered the doors to be shut. The deputation returned to the Little Church, where one of the
ministers had been reading the story of Haman and
Mordecai ; and when it was announced that the king
had given no answer, the multitude were furious.
The tumult thickened, and Lord Lindsay shouted at
the top of his voice not to separate, that their only
hope of safety was to remain and send notice to
their friends to come and assist them. Some cried,
" To bring out the wicked Haman " ; others shouted
" The sword of the Lord and Gideon ! " one of the
crowd cried, " Fy ! fy ! save yourselves, the Catholics
are coming to massacre you ! to arms, to arms ! bills
and axes." Some fancied that the king was a
prisoner, and ran to the council chamber ; others,
imagining that the ministers were being murdered,
flew to the church ; some knocked on the chamber
door and called for the president and other counsellors to be delivered up to them, that summary
punishment might be executed upon the misdoers.
The provost of the city at last arrived on the scene,
addressed the multitude, and advised them to go
quietly to their homes ; thus the uproar was quelled
without any serious mischief.

After the king's courage revived, he determined to
let the ministers and the citizens feel the weight of
his wrath. The following morning he left Edinburgh
for Linlithgow, and issued a proclamation which de-
scribed the disturbance as a treasonable uproar, and
ordered the Courts of Law to be removed from the

capital, which was an unfit place for the administration of justice. The burgesses and craftsmen saw in this move the loss of their trade, and therefore were ready to yield, and they implored his Majesty's clemency; but the only answer which he gave them was an announcement that ere long he would return to Edinburgh and let them know that he was their king. The provost was commanded to imprison the ministers, and the tumult was declared a treasonable riot. Finally the provost and magistrates were were severely punished, and a fine of 20,000 marks was imposed on the capital.

The severe punishment of the citizens of Edinburgh enabled the king to extend his power over the Church. For a time the chief ministers of the capital were silenced, and some of them fled to England. James then directed his efforts to undermine the Presbyterian polity and re-introduce Episcopacy, and he persistently pursued this line of policy to the end of his reign. He endeavoured to limit and control the action of the General Assemblies, but he effected comparatively little till after his accession to the throne of England.

Readers of Scotch history become familiar with the plots of the nobles against the Crown, and the 5th of August, 1600, was memorable for an event of this character, known as the Gowrie Conspiracy. The Earl of Gowrie of that time was the grandson of Lord Ruthven, who acted a leading part in the Riccio tragedy. It seems probable that Gowrie intended to imprison the king and rule the kingdom in his name, as had often been done before. The earl decoyed the king to his castle, and after dinner conducted him into a room in which the Master of Ruthven handled him rather roughly. But the nobles who accompanied the king came to his rescue, and after a short scuffle the master and his brother, the Earl of Gowrie, were both slain. The king insisted that all men must believe that his precious life was miraculously preserved from the hands of the two wicked brothers. He issued a mandate to change the week-day religious service in all the towns to Tuesday, the day on which the miraculous event happened ; and an Act of Parliament was passed which commanded that the 5th of August should be observed annually— " in all ages to come as a perpetual monument of their humble, hearty, and unfeigned thanks to God for His miraculous and extraordinary deliverance from the horrible and detestable murder attempted against his Majesty's most noble person."

Queen Elizabeth died on the 24th of March, 1603 ; and the same day James VI. was proclaimed her successor. For some time the English had been looking toward the rising sun ; and if he did not fulfil all the expectations of his new subjects, perhaps it was more their own fault than his, for if they had moderated their hopes and expected little, they would not have been disappointed. James began his journey on the 5th of April, and on the 6th of May, he entered London, greeted by the shouts of his English subjects.

The Scotch literature of the Reformation period is

more remarkable for its moral qualities than its intellectual ; it presents more evidence of change in the feelings and sentiments of the nation than of any display of increasing intellectual power. The writers in the Scotch dialect of the later part of the century are inferior to those of the first quarter of the century. After the Reformation there is no Scotch poet equal to Dunbar or Gavin Douglas ; the versifiers of the close of the century stand lower than those of its opening years ; the balance in conception and range of imagery is on the side of the earlier poets. If we look to the feelings and sentiments expressed in the compositions of both, the later appear in a more favourable light. The extremely coarse phrases and expressions which Dunbar and Sir David Lindsay frequently used were gradually cast aside, and a better moral tone observed. The improvement of the moral sentiments and broadening of the national sympathy were indicated in various directions—in the emphatic complaints touching the poor and the efforts to relieve them ; in the attempts to place the institution of marriage on a proper footing, to protect the life of infants, to purify the domestic circle, and to expose vice in every quarter. In short, the revolutionary waves of the sixteenth century were mainly religious and moral ; but these were soon followed by intellectual achievements and revolutions of thought.

George Buchanan wrote his poems, " History of Scotland," and " De Jure Regni apud Scotos," in Latin ; and it is necessary to notice the last work, as it was condemned and burned by the government of Scotland, when bent on a despotic policy. The " De Jure Regni," which is written in the dialogue form, appeared in 1579, and at once excited attention. The principles enunciated in it are clear and decisive, and directed against every form of tyranny. Buchanan's main argument was put in this manner : " Men were naturally formed for society, but in order to arrest

GEORGE BUCHANAN.

the internal broils that sprang up amongst them, they created kings ; and in order to restrain the power of their kings, they enacted laws. As the community is the source of legal power, it is greater than the king, and may therefore judge him ; and since the laws are intended to restrain the king in case of collision, it is for the people, not for the ruler, to interpret them. It is the duty of the king to associate himself with the law, and to govern exclusively according to its decisions. A king is one that rules by law, and in accordance with the interests of the people ; but a tyrant is one that rules by his own will, and contrary to the interests of the people. An opinion had been advanced that a king who was hampered by recognised constitutional ties might be resisted if he violated them, but that a tyrant who reigns where no constitution exists, must be always obeyed ; the latter is wrong : For the people may justly make war against such a ruler, and may pursue him till he be slain." Buchanan illustrated his views by examples drawn from history. He had also the merit of disentangling politics from the endless subtleties and puerile conceits of theologians.

In no department of human effort was the evidence of the new era more striking than in education. From an early period there were schools attached to some of the monasteries, and in some of the towns, in which Latin was taught ; and also a few places called lecture schools, in which children were taught to read the vernacular. But it was only at the Reformation that anything like adequate ideas of the importance and value of education began to be entertained. The Scotch Reformers and clergy made great and prolonged efforts to introduce and extend the means of education to the humblest classes of the people.

XII.

RESULT OF THE UNION OF THE CROWNS ON SCOTLAND.

IT was natural that James VI. should endeavour to restore Episcopacy whenever he could command the requisite power ; for he was inflexibly possessed with the idea that its establishment in Scotland was essential to the existence of the throne. With the resources of England in his hands, he continued to pursue his long cherished scheme of Church government which tended to extinguish the freedom of the people and cramp the development of their national life. Always proceeding in the underhand way which characterised this policy, he interfered with the general assemblies and controlled their action.

He summoned the leaders of the Presbyterian party, Andrew Melville, James Melville, and other six ministers, to appear at the English Court in September, 1606. His aim was to engage the ministers and the English bishops in a conference touching the superior merits of Episcopacy. He commanded the Scotch ministers to attend a course of sermons preached by four English divines—on the bishops, the supremacy of the Crown, and the absence of all authority for the office of lay elders. James himself attended several of the meetings. But it soon became manifest that the king and his bishops had utterly failed to produce any change in the convictions of the Scotch ministers. They merely heard the bishops' sermons with silent contempt ; and the service was caricatured by Andrew Melville in a Latin epigram which came under the notice of the Privy Council, and for which he was summoned to answer before that august tribunal. Melville in a moment of passion when delivering a vehement invective against the hierarchy, seized and shook the white sleeves of Bancroft, the Archbishop of Canterbury, at the same time calling them " Romish rags." For this offence he was imprisoned in the Tower of London for five years, and only obtained his liberty on the condition of living for the remainder of his life beyond the king's dominions. Melville retired to Sedan, in France, and was engaged in teaching till his death in 1620. James Melville was confined first at Newcastle, and afterwards at Berwick, but never permitted to return to Scotland ; and the other six ministers were banished to remote parts of Scotland. Such were the tactics which James VI. used to subdue the opposition to his scheme of Church government ; how far they were calculated to secure success, the sequel will show.

The king having disposed of his most energetic opponents, his supporters aided by the royal influence assumed the control of the general assemblies, and proceeded to carry into effect his Majesty's injunctions. And the Scotch Parliament enacted anything which the king commanded. Thus Episcopacy was restored in 1610; though in many congregations the Presbyterian form of worship was retained, as a majority of the people were opposed to the change. But James wanted to introduce five articles of his own, which enjoined that the communion should always be received in a kneeling posture; that in cases of sickness the communion should be administered in private houses; that baptism in similar circumstances should be administered; that holydays should be appointed for the commemoration of the birth, passion, and resurrection of Christ; and that children should be brought to the bishop and blessed. These ceremonies are known in history as "the five articles of Perth." But they were inconsistent with the historic basis of the Reformed Church of Scotland, and the majority of the people were bitterly opposed to them.

James insisted that his articles should be enforced on the people. He was always exhorting and threatening in vain; nonconforming ministers were imprisoned and banished without effect; and in spite of all his efforts many of the conforming ministers' churches began to be deserted, and they were left to declaim against schism and rebellion to empty benches.

King James died on the 27th of March, 1625, at the age of fifty nine. Though naturally timid, he was vindictive, and accessible to the most fulsome flattery; he was extremely conceited—a weak feature of his character much fed by the excessive flattery of the English bishops. Of his kingly prerogatives he had the most extravagant ideas. In literature he was a pedant. It cannot be recorded that his policy was beneficial to his native country.

James VI. was succeeded by his son, Charles I. In October, 1626, he issued a revocation of all grants of lands by the Crown since the Reformation. It was intended for the benefit of the bishops and the clergy, and to remedy some evils connected with tithes. But it aroused violent feelings among the nobles whose interests it threatened to invade. The king had resolved to fight a hard battle, and firmly pursued his end. He found it necessary to limit the scope of his measure, and raised processes to reduce the grants on legal grounds. Still, this caused much alarm, and a deputation from the nobles went to London to treat with the king. After a warm discussion, a commission was appointed to examine the whole subject, in January, 1627. The commissioners proceeded with the investigation, and prosecutions were commenced against all who refused to accede to the proposals of the Crown. At last a compromise was effected. The Church lands and the property in dispute were to remain in the hands of those who held them, under the condition of paying a proportion as rents to the Crown ; while the Crown also insisted on a right of feudal superiority, whereby additional dues would fall to the public revenue. The tithes were adjusted thus :—The landowner obtained liberty to extinguish the right of levying tithes on his property by the payment of a sum calculated at nine years' purchase ; if he failed to exercise this option, then the tithe in kind was to be commuted into a rent-charge, and from this was to

be deducted the stipend payable to the parish ministers, and an annuity reserved to the Crown. The
adjustment of the tithes which was sanctioned by
Parliament in 1633, proved a beneficial measure to
the nation, as it extinguished a large class of vexatious
disputes between landowners and titheowners, between
tenants of land and titheowners, and between the
ministers and their flocks.

Still many of the great nobles only surrendered
their full claims to the Church lands with a grudge
which long embittered their minds, and predisposed
them to join in the struggle against the king which
subsequently ensued. They feared that he might yet
attempt further encroachments upon their landed
rights and privileges.

In 1633, Charles I. crossed the border and entered
Edinburgh, and was crowned at Holyrood on the
18th of June. He was exceedingly anxious to
complete the scheme of Church polity which his
father had begun, and proceeded to treat all difficulties with an imperious hand. His presence and
power overawed opposition for a time, and preparations were made for composing a new book of
canons and a liturgy. The canons, as finally revised
by Laud and the Bishops of London and Norwich,
were ratified by the king in May, 1635, and pro-
mulgated by the king in 1636. Charles announced
his will touching the canons in the following terms :
"We do, not only by our royal prerogative and
supreme authority in causes ecclesiastical, ratify and
confirm by these our letters patent, the said canons
and constitutions, and everything contained in them ;

but likewise we command, by our royal authority, the same to be diligently observed and executed, by all our loving subjects of that kingdom, in all points, . . . according to this our will and pleasure, hereby expressed and declared." The bishops and all persons in authority were commanded to enforce the observance of the canons under severe penalties. These canons placed the whole internal life of the Church in the hands of the bishops.

The canons had little resemblance to any Scotch ecclesiastical rules subsequent to the Reformation. Such was the king's disregard of the national feeling and his blind confidence in the efficacy of the royal supremacy; he imagined that he had only to command what he pleased and the people would obey him. Acting on this vain assumption, Charles signed a warrant to the Privy Council on the 18th of October, 1636, which contained his instructions touching the introduction of the new liturgy. It ordered the Council to proclaim to the nation that the liturgy must be adopted; the bishops and clergy were commanded to enforce its observance by condign censure and punishment, and two copies of it were to be procured for the use of every parish in the kingdom. In compliance with the king's command, the Council in December issued a proclamation ordering all the people to conform to the new liturgy.

The nation was soon in a ferment. A suspicion arose amongst the people that Roman Catholicism was to be reintroduced. They had already yielded much to the king, but the limit of their passive obedience was passed. They affirmed that the king had no right to impose a liturgy on them; and they asserted that it was little better than a mass-book. The royal proclamation ordered the new liturgy to be observed in all the churches on Easter, 1637, but the authorities postponed it, which merely heightened the feeling against it. The bishops arranged that the public reading of the liturgy should begin in Edinburgh on Sunday the 23rd of July; and this was intimated in all the churches of the city on the previous Sunday.

On the appointed day preparations were made to celebrate the introduction of the new service in the most imposing style. In the historic Church of St. Giles, the two archbishops and other bishops, the members of the Privy Council, and the magistrates in their robes, attended in the forenoon to grace the proceedings. The Bishop of Edinburgh was to preach and the dean to read the service. A large congregation had assembled, but they looked restless and wistful. The dean had scarcely begun to read when confused cries arose. As he proceeded, the clamour became louder and the prayers could not be heard. The people started to their feet and the church was a scene of hideous uproar. The voices of the women were loudest; some cried "Woe, woe me!" others shouted that "they were bringing in popery!" and instantly the stools were thrown at the dean and the Bishop of Edinburgh. The Archbishop of St. Andrews and the Lords of the Council interposed, but in vain; the tumult continued till the magistrates came from their seats in the gallery and with extreme difficulty thrust out the unruly members. The dean read the service, and the bishop preached with barred doors. But the crowd stood around the church in a state of vehement excitement, rapping at the doors and throwing stones at the windows, and shouting " Popery, popery ! " When the bishops came out of the church the multitude attacked Bishop Lindsay, and he narrowly escaped with his life.

Similar disturbances occurred in the other churches of the capital, though less violent. In Greyfriars Church the bishop was forced to stop reading the service. The excitement spread rapidly and became intense ; and the liturgy was everywhere spurned. In the face of this heated feelin g the authorities were powerless. On the 4th of August, the Privy Council were commanded by the king to punish all the persons concerned in the disturbance, and to support the bishops and clergy in establishing the liturgy. The Council resolved that another attempt should be made to use it on Sunday the 13th of August ; but when this day came it was not tried in the churches of Edinburgh, because readers could not be got to officiate. Thus the curtain was drawn, and the first scene of the long tragic drama enacted.

XIII.

THE COVENANTING CONFLICT.

Two lines of action were open to the king, either to withdraw the liturgy unconditionally, or at once to overwhelm all opposition. Charles I. was not inclined to adopt the first. Though quite unprepared to enforce the second, he clung to it, and only slowly and with painful difficulty became aware that his power was not commensurate with his will. The national feeling was imperfectly understood in London. The king himself had merely looked at a few unimportant circumstances on the surface of society, and thence concluded that the Scots would offer little opposition to the introduction of the liturgy. The tone of Charles' dispatches clearly indicated his view of the matter, which was this :— Every one in Scotland had done something wrong or neglected to do what should have been done ; so his Majesty alone, under God, was right, and therefore his will must be obeyed.

The agitation and excitement increased throughout the kingdom, and the Government were utterly powerless. Petitions against the liturgy began to be circulated, and Mr. Alexander Henderson, minister of Leuchars, in Fife, presented one to the Privy Council on the 23rd of August, 1637. This petition gave the following reasons for rejecting the liturgy:— (1) Because it is not warranted by the authority of the General Assembly, nor by any Act of Parliament; (2) Because the liberties of the Church and form of religion and worship received at the Reformation, and universally practised since, were warranted by the Acts of the General Assembly and by several Acts of Parliament; (3) Because the Church of Scotland was a free Church, and her own ministers were best able to discern what was in harmony with the Reformation, and best calculated to promote the good of the people; (4) Because it was notorious what disputes and trouble had arisen in the Church about a few of the many ceremonies in this liturgy; (5) Because since the Reformation the people have always been taught a different doctrine, and they would not likely be willing to agree to such changes, even though their pastors were willing to submit. The Council informed the king of the discontent and the clamour against the liturgy, and agreed to let the matter rest till further instructed by his Majesty.

The king replied on the 10th of September, and expressed his displeasure that they had not caused the liturgy to be read, nor inflicted condign punishment on those who had raised the tumult. He insisted that each bishop should cause it to be observed in his own diocese.

On the 20th of September, many petitions against

the liturgy were presented to the Council. The movement was fast gaining strength; twenty nobles, many of the gentry, and the chief men of the towns had joined it. A great number of people assembled in Edinburgh, and the Earl of Sutherland presented a general petition to the Council, in name of the nobility, the ministers, and the burgesses. The

COMMON SEAL OF EDINBURGH.

Council were perplexed and hesitated; at last they declined to answer the petitions till they got instructions from the king. They informed the king of the state of matters; and on the 9th of October, he replied that he had postponed an answer to the petitions.

In the middle of October, a greater number of people than before met in Edinburgh, with the aim of inducing the magistrates to join the movement, and to await the king's answer Fresh petitions from two hundred parishes were presented ; but a plain and wise answer from the king might still have dissipated all alarm. On the 17th of October, the king's answer was announced in the form of three proclamations at the cross of Edinburgh. The first intimated that nothing would be done that day touching religious matters, and the petitioners were commanded to leave the capital within twenty-four hours ; the second ordered the Government and the Courts of Law to remove to Linlithgow ; and the third denounced a book which was popular, " A Dispute against the English Popish Ceremonies obtruded upon the Church of Scotland," all copies of which were ordered to be brought to the Council and publicly burned.

The people were deeply offended, and at once resolved to disobey the proclamations, and not to separate till they established a rallying point. Next morning, when the Bishop of Galloway was going to the Council-house, a mob attacked him and pursued him to the door. The crowd surrounded the Council-house and demanded that the obnoxious lords should surrender. The Council despatched a messenger to the magistrates to ask their help, but they were in the same plight as the Council. A part of the mob gathered around the town-house, and, entering the lobbies, threatened that, unless the magistrates joined the citizens in opposing the liturgy, they would burn the building. When this became known to the Council, the Treasurer and the Earl of Wigton forced their way to the town-house. After a brief consultation, the magistrates agreed to do all in their power to disperse the crowds, and announced to the seething multitude that they had acceded to the demands of the people. The Treasurer and his friends now thought that they might venture to return to the Council-house; but the moment they appeared on the street, they were assailed with hootings and jeers. Then a rush was made, and the Treasurer was thrown to the ground; his hat, cloak, and staff of office were torn from him, and he was in danger of being trodden to death. Some of his companions, however, got him to his feet, and the pressure of the crowd half carried him and his friends to the Council-house door. In a short time the magistrates joined the Council, and all the authorities were beset, and many of them trembled. At last it was resolved to send for the nobles who had already announced themselves opposed to the liturgy, and by their exertions the crowd was dispersed, and the counsellors got safely to their homes.

Before separating, the opposition party agreed to meet again on the 15th of November. In the interval they exerted themselves to the utmost to secure a large meeting of the people, to await for an answer to their former petitions.

The Privy Council greatly feared a repetition of the tumults, and held a conference with the leaders of the petitioners. The nobles on the side of the petitioners maintained their right to meet and to present their grievances; but to obviate all cause of complaint, they said that their party were ready to act through representatives. The Council agreed ; and the opposition party appointed four permanent committees. The first comprised all the nobles who had joined the movement ; the second consisted of two representatives from each county ; the third embraced one minister from each presbytery ; and the fourth included one or two deputies from each borough. These committees sat at different tables in the parliament-house (hence in history they were called the Tables), and acting together they represented the nation. For effective action and business each of the committees elected four representatives, and these united formed a select deliberative body of sixteen members, appointed to sit constantly in Edinburgh, with instructions to assemble the larger body when any emergency arose. At first they only took charge of the petitions, and urged them on the attention of the Government ; but they shortly began to form proposals for the party, to assume the functions of government, and the control of affairs passed into their hands.

On the 21st of December, 1637, the representatives of the Tables appeared before the Privy Council and demanded that their petitions should be heard. Lord Loudon boldly stated their grievances. As the bishops were the chief delinquents and directly interested parties, it was claimed that they should not be allowed to sit as judges upon the matters in dispute between the Government and the petitioners. The Council remitted the whole matter for the determination of the king.

THE EARL OF LOUDON.

In the beginning of 1638, Traquair, the Lord Treasurer, was called to London. He found that the king was not only extremely ignorant of the state of affairs, but was unwilling to listen to information about the difficulties which he had caused. Some consultation was held concerning what should be done, but any idea of yielding to the opinions of the Scots could not be entertained by the king; and it was resolved to adhere to the liturgy and the Court of High Commission, to ignore and condemn all that had been objected against them, as the royal supremacy must be maintained. Charles took the responsibility of the liturgy on himself; and the Treasurer returned with his instructions in the middle of February.

A proclamation in accordance with the king's conclusions was issued on the 19th of February. But the representatives of the Tables immediately protested that they should still have a right to petition the king; that they would not recognise the bishops as judges in any Court; that they should not incur any loss for non-observance of such canons and proclamations as were contrary to the Acts of Parliament and of the General Assembly; and that if any disturbance should arise, it should not be imputed to them.

The crisis had come. The opposition party felt that they could not recede, and therefore it was requisite to look to the future. Their only hope of successfully resisting the king was to unite on some easily understood principle, which should touch the sympathies and the religious emotions of the people. At this stage an old custom suggested itself as appropriate to the emergency ; it was proposed, as in bygone days, that every adherent of the cause should be bound as one man by a solemn Covenant. The framing of the Covenant was entrusted to the Rev. Alexander Henderson, and Johnston of Warriston, an advocate ; and the Earls of Rothes, Loudon, and Balmerino, were selected to revise it. This national Covenant consisted of three parts :—The first was a copy of the negative confession of 1581 ; the second contained a summary of the Acts of Parliament which condemned Roman Catholicism, and ratified the Reformed Church ; and the third was the new Covenant, by which the subscribers swore in the name of the " Lord their God," that they would remain in the profession of their religion ; that they would defend it to the utmost of their power from all errors ; that they would stand by the king's person in support of the true religion, the liberties, and the laws of the kingdom ; and that they would stand by each other in defence of the same against all persons.

When everything was prepared it was resolved to inaugurate the Covenant in Edinburgh on the 28th of February, 1638. A multitude of the people assembled in the Greyfriars Church and Churchyard, and they were warmly addressed touching the preservation of their religion, their duty to God, and to their country. At two o'clock the Earls of Rothes and Loudon, Henderson and Dickson ministers, and Johnston of Warriston, appeared with the Covenant. The Earl of Sutherland was the first who signed it, and then all crowded toward the table and added their names. When those in the Church had signed, it was taken

14

out to the churchyard and placed on a flat gravestone. There the enthusiasm reached its height, men and women were equally eager to subscribe their names, and the work proceeded till every inch of the long roll of parchment was covered. At last night closed the scene.

The following day the Covenant was circulated in Edinburgh, and copies sent throughout the kingdom. Everywhere great efforts were made to arouse the enthusiasm of the people, and in two months nearly all the inhabitants of the country had signed the Covenant. The Privy Council were sitting in Stirling when the Covenant appeared, and were greatly embarrassed. After two days' deliberation they agreed to send the Lord Justice Clerk to London to tell the king that the whole nation was in a state of vehement excitement. In April several members of the Privy Council were called to the Court, and some of the bishops were already there, so that Charles I. had a good opportunity of learning the real state of Scotland. The Scotch counsellors suggested soothing remedies, and the state of matters was earnestly discussed. At last the king called to his closet the Archbishops of Canterbury and St. Andrews, the Bishops of Galloway, Brechin, and Ross, and the Marquis of Hamilton ; and measures of repression were adopted. The king announced that Hamilton would proceed to Scotland as High Commissioner, with power to settle the troubles. Charles' instructions to Hamilton were signed on the 16th of May, 1638, and extended to twenty-eight articles, of which the concluding one was in these terms :—" If you cannot, by the means prescribed by us, bring back the refractory and seditious to due obedience, we do not only give you authority, but command all hostile acts to be used against them, they having deserved to be used in no other way by us, but as a rebellious people ; for the doing whereof we will not only save you harmless, but account it acceptable service to us." A proclamation in accord with these instructions was prepared, which Hamilton was to issue in Scotland.

The marquis arrived early in June, and soon found that his instructions were utterly useless. He did not venture to publish the royal proclamation as he had no means to enforce it. He informed the king that he should either concede all the demands of his subjects or be prepared to suppress the movement by force. The king replied that his preparations were progressing, and meantime he told Hamilton to flatter the Covenanters with any hopes he pleased, so as to gain time until he should be in a position to suppress them. For, said Charles, " I will rather die than yield to their impertinent and damnable demands." Other communications passed between the king and Hamilton, and the result is thus stated by Charles : " I will only say that so long as this Covenant is in force, whether it be with or without explanations, I have no more power in Scotland than as a Duke of Venice, which I will rather die than suffer ; yet I command the giving ear to their explanations or to anything to win time."

Hamilton saw that he could do nothing to restore the confidence of the nation, and he returned to London. Before leaving he issued, in an amended form, the king's proclamation, which had now assumed an apologetic strain in defence of the king's action ; but it had no effect on the Covenanters. During Hamilton's absence they were intently engaged in completing their organisation.

After some deliberation the king, with the advice of Laud, issued new instructions to Hamilton. He was empowered under limits to summon a general assembly and a parliament. He was to arrange that the bishops should have votes in the Assembly ; to protest against the abolition of bishops, but might permit them to be tried if accused of definite crimes ; and to insist that no laymen should vote in the election of ministers to the Assembly.

When Hamilton returned to Scotland on the 8th of August, he found that the demands of the Covenanters had risen, and that they would not agree to the limitations which he proposed. They wanted a free assembly, and told Hamilton that it might be called by themselves without waiting for the king's authority. Hamilton received new instructions, and the weakness and folly of Charles's policy became painfully manifest.

The nation was wistfully looking forward to the General Assembly. The leaders of the Covenanters were actively engaged in preparing for its proper constitution. Their organisation was so complete and effective that the supporters of Episcopacy gave up the contest in despair, but the king clung to it after all reasonable hope of success was utterly gone. As the day of the meeting of the Assembly approached, men began to flock into Glasgow from all quarters of the kingdom. It met on the 21st of November, 1638, in the Cathedral of Glasgow. The Covenanters insisted that the first requisite to constitute the Assembly was to elect a moderator; but Hamilton, the royal commissioner, argued that a moderator should not be elected till the commissions of the members were examined. When it appeared that he would be defeated, he proposed to read a paper, in the name of the bishops, against the Assembly, but this was met with shouts of dissent. A stormy debate ensued, followed by protests and counter protests, which continued till every one was wearied. Alexander Henderson, minister of Leuchars, was elected moderator, and Johnston of Warriston, appointed clerk of the Assembly. The bishops' declinature of the Assembly's authority was again urged by Hamilton, and read by the clerk amid jeers and laughter. Hamilton spoke and argued on its importance, and parts of it were debated. The moderator then put the question, Whether the Assembly found itself a competent judge of the bishops? Hamilton rose and said, if the Assembly proceeded to censure the offices of the bishops he must immediately withdraw, as the king's sanction could not be given to it. Able and animated speeches were delivered on the freedom of the Assembly, to which Hamilton replied by arguing that the election of the members had been controlled by the Tables. At last, in the king's name, he dissolved the Assembly and departed. But a protest was read, a vote taken, and the Assembly resolved to continue its sittings.

It proceeded rapidly with its work. All the acts

of the Assemblies since 1605 were annulled.   The
book of canons, the liturgy, the High Commission, and
Episcopacy were condemned.   The bishops were
tried, convicted, and condemned, though none of
them were present.   They had always allied themselves with the despotic tendencies of the Crown ;
they were the mere tools of the king, and belonged
to him, not to the people ; they were intended to be,
and to the utmost limits of their power had been,
the pliant instruments of the royal will and pleasure,
not the servants of the nation.   The presbyterian
polity and organisation was restored.   Acts were
passed touching education, and many other important
subjects.   The Assembly closed its work by appoint-
ing its next meeting to be held at Edinburgh in July,
1639.

After the conclusions of the Assembly, civil war
became inevitable, and both sides were preparing
for the conflict.   General Alexander Leslie, who had
acquired much experience, and attained to rank in
the German wars, was appointed leader of the Covenanting army.   He soon organised a force and
equipped it for the field.   The Covenanters seized
the castles of Edinburgh, Dumbarton, and other
strongholds.

Charles I. had ordered his army to muster at York,
in April, 1639.   He proposed to lead the army in
person, and sent his fleet into the Firth of Forth.
But ere the king arrived at York, the whole of
Scotland was in the hands of the Covenanters.   In
May, the Covenanting army was encamped at
Dunse Law ; and Charles posted his army on the

opposite side of the Tweed. The two armies watched each other for several days, and both seemed unwilling to strike. The Covenanters knew their advantages, but if the king had honestly granted their reasonable requests without battle, they would have been glad. An arrangement was made, by which the religious matters in dispute were to be referred to the General Assembly and to Parliament. Peace was proclaimed on the 18th of June. But mutual confidence between the king and the Scots was not restored.

Charles trifled with the serious matters in dispute, and the causes of dissension were intensified. He had determined to chastise the Scots, and summoned his English parliament, which met in April, 1640. A majority of Parliament refused to grant supplies till they obtained the redress of their grievances; but rather than yield, the king in anger dissolved the House of Commons. Difficulties now gathered thickly around him. The Scotch Parliament met in June, and repealed all the Acts which permitted churchmen to sit and vote in Parliament. It enacted that a parliament should meet every three years, and appointed a permanent committee of members to act when Parliament was not sitting.

The Covenanters were engaged in organising their army in the spring and summer of 1640. Under Leslie they marched southward, crossed the Tweed on the 21st of August, advanced and forced the passage of the Tyne, and on the 30th took possession of Newcastle. Charles with an army of 18,000 men was encamped at York; and the Cove-

FLAG OF THE COVENANTERS.

nanters petitioned him to listen to their grievances, and with the concurrence of the English Parliament to conclude a lasting peace. At the same time a number of English nobles petitioned the king to summon a parliament, and his difficulties daily increased. He offered to negotiate with the Covenanters, and summoned the English Parliament to meet at Westminster, on the 3rd of November—a parliament afterwards known as "the Long Parliament." Parties appointed by the king and the Covenanters met at Ripon, and agreed that the Scotch army should remain inactive at Newcastle. Thus matters stood for some time; and the place of negotiating was transferred to London. After long treating, terms of peace were agreed to, and ratified in August, 1641.

At this time Charles, wishing to please the Scots, resolved to visit Scotland, and arrived in Edinburgh in August. Parliament being then in session, the king attended a meeting, and delivered a speech. He touched on the difficulties which had arisen between him and his subjects, of his anxiety to settle them, and of his love for his native country which had caused him to face many dangers to be present at that time. He referred to the royal power transmitted to him through one hundred and eight descents, which they had so often professed to maintain. Charles in concluding said, "The end of my coming is to perfect all that I have promised; and withal, to quiet those distractions which have and may fall out amongst you; and this I am resolved fully and cheerfully to do; for I can do nothing with more cheerfulness than to give my people content and satisfaction."

The Covenanters might have been satisfied as they had obtained all that they demanded. But other views had entered into their minds, and they now desired to give their principles a wider range of application. Charles seems to have imagined that he would be able to overcome the English, if he could pacify the Scots ; and he left Edinburgh for England on the 18th of November. The breach between him and his English subjects was constantly widening. He was forced to leave London, and removed his court to York, in the spring of 1642.

Communications passed between the English Parliamentary party and the Covenanters. The General Assembly met at Edinburgh on the 2nd of August, 1643 when Sir Thomas Hope, the Lord Advocate, appeared as royal commissioner. On the 7th, four commissioners from the Long Parliament landed at Leith, among whom was Sir Henry Vane ; and in a few days they were introduced to the Assembly. They said that they warmly appreciated the energy of the Covenanters in extinguishing popery ; that they were anxious to have this reform completed in England ; that they had already abolished the High Commission and Episcopacy, expelled the bishops from the House of Lords, and summoned an assembly of divines which had met at Westminster. Therefore, they entreated the Covenanters to assist their brethren in England, who were so hard pressed by the king's forces, and exposed to the utmost peril. The proposal was much discussed, and there was difference of opinion in the Assembly. Some proposed to mediate between the king and Parliament, and not commit themselves further ; but the opposite views of Johnston of Warriston and others prevailed, and it was agreed to assist the leaders of the Long Parliament. There was much debate on the tenor of the agreement. The English proposed a civil league, the Scots would listen to nothing but a religious covenant. The English suggested that toleration should be given to the Independents, but the Scots would tolerate nothing but Presbyterianism in both kingdoms. After a long and characteristic debate, "the Solemn League and Covenant" was placed before the Assembly, and unanimously adopted. All the parties to this Covenant bound themselves to preserve the Reformed religion in Scotland ; to work for the reformation of religion in England and Ireland ; to struggle to the utmost to bring the Churches in the three kingdoms to a uniformity of faith, of polity, and form of worship ; to endeavour to extinguish popery, episcopacy, heresy, schism, and everything opposed to sound doctrine; to preserve the rights of the Parliaments and the liberties of the three kingdoms; to preserve and defend the king's person, and his just power, authority, and greatness unimpaired.

A copy of the Solemn League and Covenant was carried to London. On the 22nd of September, 1643, the members of the House of Commons, the House of Lords, and the Westminster Assembly of divines, all signed it ; and afterwards it was signed by many in every county of England. Its immediate effect was that a Scotch army of twenty thousand men crossed the Tweed to assist the Parliamentary forces.

The government of Scotland was managed by the committee of Parliament and the commission of the General Assembly. But the nation was not all of one mind, and some of the nobles formed a royalist party. The Earl of Montrose had been for years an ardent Covenanter, but he turned to the king's side, and was commissioned to raise the royal standard in August, 1644. He was soon at the head of three thousand men, a part of whom were Irish. His short career and exploits have often been detailed, and it is needless to repeat them, as his victories had little effect on the main stream of history.

Since the battle of Marston Moor, in July, 1644, in which the Scots under David Leslie were engaged, the king's cause had been falling lower and lower. At last driven to despair, he fled to the Scotch army at Newcastle, in May, 1646. The Long Parliament demanded that the Scots should surrender him, but they declined. They were eager to extend Presbyterianism to England, and attempted to negotiate with the king. He was asked to abolish Episcopacy, to ratify the proceedings of the Westminster Assembly of divines, and to sign the Covenant himself. But Charles on his conscience declined, as he believed in the Divine right of Episcopacy.

The Long Parliament announced that the Scottish army was no longer required in England, and the Scots replied that they were ready to retire as soon as their arrears were paid. In the matter of pay there was a serious difficulty, for between the amount claimed by the Scots, and the amount admitted by the English as due, there was a difference of more than half a million. The difference between the two accounts mainly related to provisions which the English charged in full, but the greater part of which the Scots asserted never came to them, it having been taken by the enemy, part lost and part damaged. The sum claimed by the Scots was nearly two millions, of which they acknowledged the receipt of seven hundred thousand, but which by the English mode of reckoning amounted to fourteen hundred thousand ; thus leaving seven hundred thousand of a difference between the sum claimed by the Scotch, and the sum admitted as due by the Long Parliament. A long wrangle between the parties ensued. Every item in the account was minutely examined and hotly debated, till at last the Scots offered to accept a gross sum of five hundred thousand pounds. On this there was a long and vehement debate in the Long Parliament ; finally the English agreed to pay four hundred thousand pounds, one fourth before the Scots left Newcastle, and the remainder by instalments.

The Long Parliament resolved to dispose of the king's person as it thought fit ; the Scots objected, but in vain. The English determinedly insisted that they must have the king. At last the Scotch Parliament consented to let him go to Holmby, in Northamptonshire, "there to remain till he give satisfaction to both kingdoms ; but, in the interim, that there be no harm, injury, or violence done to his person." On the 23rd of January, 1647, the English commissioners received the king at Newcastle; and on the 30th the Scotch army withdrew.

The narrative of the trial of Charles I., belongs to English history, and has often been admirably told. The Scotch Parliament, through its commissioners in London, remonstrated against any injury to the king's person, and reaffirmed that it was on this condition they consented to part with him; but his fate was decreed. On the 30th of January, 1649, he was beheaded before his own palace at Whitehall. It was Charles's lot to be educated in a one-sided and pernicious political belief. He was incapable of distinguishing between his moral and political rights, which led his comparatively narrow mind to assume and to maintain that his political position gave him an unquestionable right to dictate to his subjects the form of their worship. He forced himself into trying circumstances, and found himself face to face with great political and religious difficulties, which he failed to appreciate and surmount.

XIV.

CHARLES II. THE KINGDOM UNDER CROMWELL.

PARLIAMENT was sitting when tidings of the king's execution reached Scotland, and on the 5th of February, 1649, his son, Charles II. was proclaimed king. The national sentiment of the Scots inclined to monarchical government, their Covenants recognized it, and they had no idea of establishing a republic. Two days after the proclamation, Parliament expressed the sentiment of the nation in an Act which declared that before the young king was admitted to the exercise of his functions, he should sign and swear the national Covenant, and the Solemn League and Covenant; that he should consent to the Acts of Parliament enjoining these Covenants; and that he should never attempt to change any of them. Further, that he should dismiss the counsel of all those opposed to the Covenants and religion; that he should give satisfaction to Parliament in everything requisite for settling a lasting peace; and that he should consent that all civil matters should be determined by Parliament, and ecclesiastical matters by the General Assembly.

On the 6th of March Parliament commissioned the
Earl of Cassillis and others to proceed to Holland
and offer the Crown to the young king on the conditions indicated in the preceding paragraph. But
Charles declined to commit himself, and no arrangement was made. Early in the spring of 1650, treating
with the prince was resumed on the same conditions.
After some conversation Charles agreed to the terms
of the Scots, and, embarking for the home of his
fathers, arrived at the mouth of the Spey on the
23rd of June. There he signed the Covenant, landed
the following day, and thence proceeded southward.
The Scots determined that the king should conform
to the national principles.

The Covenanters were bitterly opposed to the
party at the head of the English Commonwealth, and
this party were deeply offended at the movement in
Scotland on behalf of the young king. Accordingly,
Cromwell entered Scotland in July, and advanced to
the vicinity of Edinburgh ; but was unable to take
it. He retired to Dunbar, where a severe battle
was fought on the 3rd of September, in which the
Covenanters were completely defeated. Shortly after
Cromwell seized Edinburgh, and in the middle of
October was master of the south-eastern counties.

The Scots became more divided among themselves,
as in the heat of conflict there had arisen several
minute differences of opinion and sentiment on the
burning questions of the time, which each party
maintained with characteristic determination. There
were three parties in Scotland. The Government,
with the Marquis of Argyle at its head, consisted of

the committee of Parliament and the commission of the General Assembly ; and the body of the clergy who supported the Government and the resolutions of Parliament, were called the Resolutioners. They seconded the efforts of the Government to defend the kingdom by all available means. Then, the more extreme party of Covenanters, who maintained that though the king had signed the Covenant, yet on his part it was a mere sham ; and this section were called Protesters. Apart from both the presbyterian parties, stood the extreme Royalist party, who numbered in their ranks the Marquis of Huntly, the Earls of Athole, Seaforth, and others ; these were open enemies of the Covenants.

In spite of the internal commotion the king was crowned at Scone on the 1st of January, 1651 ; and he again swore to maintain the national Covenant, and the Solemn League and Covenant. As the Scots were unable to repulse the English army, they resolved on a raid across the border. Charles II. accompanied the Scotch army into England ; but Cromwell with a part of his force followed him. A battle ensuing at Worcester on the 3rd of September, the Royalists were defeated, and the king escaped to the Continent.

After this, General Monk undertook the reduction of Scotland, and executed it more thoroughly than Edward I. On the 28th of August, the committee of Parliament were surprised and captured in Angus, with five members of the commission of the General Assembly, and they were all sent prisoners to England. The Lowlands submitted to the English

15

army ; but some resistance continued to be offered
by the Royalists in the Highlands. They also were
shortly subdued, and the country reduced to order.

When the nation was subdued, the Government of
the Commonwealth was disposed to treat Scotland
justly, according to its own view of the necessities of
the case. The aim of Cromwell and his associates, so
far as it appears, was to amalgamate the two nations
into one republic. Cromwell made a bold attempt
to extinguish the feudal power of the Scotch nobles.
He placed twenty garrisons in the kingdom, and kept
an army of from seven thousand to nine thousand
men in the country. The taxes imposed to support
this force pressed hard on the Scots ; but then peace
and security reigned, which was not to be lightly
estimated.

The most successful part of the incorporating
scheme was the adoption of free trade between the
two countries. This was a great advantage to the
Scots.

Cromwell placed the civil administration of Scotland in the hands of a council of nine men, most of
whom were Englishmen. The Court of Session was
superseded by a supreme commission of justice,
consisting of seven judges, four English and three
Scotch. They had to deal with the attempted change
in the laws, already indicated, the abolition of the
feudal system, and the adjustment of the many
entangled interests thence arising. A collection of
their decisions is preserved, and they are marked by
good sense and careful work.

By an ordinance of 1654, another body of seven

men were constituted trustees of forfeited and seques-
trated estates. Their duties were to look after the
rents and the revenues of the many Scotch nobles
and lairds whose estates had been seized by the
Government for offences arising out of the conquest.
They were instructed to pay creditors, and to give
allowances to the wives, the widows, and the children
of the original owners of the estates.

In 1656, Baillie said : "Our State is in a very
silent condition. Strong garrisons over all the land,
and a great army, both of horse and foot, for which
there is no service at all. Our nobles lying in prisons,
and under forfeitures or debts, private or public, are
for the most part either broken or breaking."

On the 3rd of September, 1658, Cromwell died.
Though the supreme power which he had won by his
energy passed on to his son Richard, this man was
unequal for the task imposed on him, and in a few
months retired into private life. The government of
the three kingdoms fell into the hands of the leaders
of the armies, and they then began a scramble
for the summit of power ; but Oliver's mantle
had not descended upon any of them. So the
traditions and sentiments associated with the glory
of the throne and the monarchy were soon in the
ascendant. Many circumstances aided General Monk,
and he assumed the guidance of the issue. He was
at the head of the army in Scotland, and having
collected his forces, he carefully prepared to march
into England. He called a meeting of the chief men
and advised them to preserve the internal peace of
the kingdom ; and they aided him with a sum of

money. In November, 1659, he began his march and entered England in the beginning of 1660. After various moves, Monk declared in favour of a free parliament, which met in March, and resolved to recall the king.   And Charles II. entered London, on the 29th of May, amid the applause of the people.

XV.

RESTORATION. PERSECUTION.

THE Restoration in both divisions of the island was a reactionary movement, which arose partly from the customary notions of the people ; while amongst the nobility the traditional feelings associated with the Crown were interwoven with their own privileges of rank, of wealth, and of power, in the social organisation and the constitution of the monarchy. Under the Commonwealth the hereditary nobles had suffered enormously. They had been deprived of power, harassed, imprisoned, banished, and many of them ruined. With the hope of escaping from this depression, the Lords and Commons of England committed themselves to the discretion of Charles II. But what had happened could not be completely reversed nor the recollection of it extinguished.

Scotland suffered far more from the Restoration than England. It was an easy matter to turn the Church of England into her original groove. The task undertaken by the Government of Charles II. in Scotland was more difficult ; it was an attempt to turn aside the current of religious thought and sentiment sprung from the Reformation of 1560. The attempt failed ; although everything was done to crush the spirit of the people and to extinguish their liberty.

Many of the Scotch nobles flocked to London, eager to present their claims for posts in the new government of the kingdom. The civil war and the subjection of the nation under Cromwell had rendered them extremely poor and demoralised ; so they were more alert than ever to grasp at anything that seemed likely to advance their interest. Therefore, they elected to follow the king and the Court in whatever might be proposed ; principles and convictions were cast aside with scorn ; Covenants, equity, and justice, might go to the wall, but Charles II. must be upheld. The Earl of Rothes was appointed President of the Council, Glencairn Chancellor, Crawford Treasurer, and Sir John Fletcher, Lord Advocate. And it was agreed that the committee of Parliament held at Stirling in 1650, should resume the government.

The committee of Parliament arrested the Rev. James Guthrie and other ministers, and imprisoned them in the castle of Edinburgh. Public meetings were prohibited and petitioning was suppressed. The ministers were specially warned to be careful of their language in sermons, prayers, and conversation. On the 8th of July, 1560, the Marquis of Argyle was seized in London and lodged in the Tower ; at the same time orders were issued to arrest Johnston of Warriston, and other gentlemen.

Parliament met on the 1st of January, 1661, and

the Earl of Middleton appeared as royal commissioner. The new parliament immediately proceeded to business, and passed Acts in accord with the inclination of Charles II. The grand achievement of the session was an Act which repealed all the legislation of Scotland from 1633 to the Restoration. Thus Presbyterianism ceased to be the established religion of the nation. Some of the presbyteries and synods warmly protested against the re-introduction of Episcopacy ; but in many instances they were forcibly dissolved, and in others the party on the side of the Government ordered the meetings to be cleared of rebels, and by such means the opposition was stifled.

The Government sacrificed a few victims as a warning to others. The Marquis of Argyle was placed at the bar of Parliament and accused of treason. After a long trial, he was convicted, condemned, and executed at Edinburgh on the 27th of May, 1661. The Rev. James Guthrie, minister of Stirling, was summoned before Parliament and accused of treason. The chief points of the charge against him were that he contrived and presented to the committee of Parliament a document called " The Western Remonstrance," that he was the author of a pamphlet entitled " The Causes of God's Wrath," and that he had declined his Majesty's jurisdiction. Such charges might have been brought against any one. But Guthrie was condemned and executed. Other ministers were accused before Parliament and sentenced to undergo various punishments. Johnston of Warriston had escaped to the Continent, but he was condemned in his absence. He was afterwards taken

in France, conveyed to Scotland, and executed at
Edinburgh.

The privy council was reconstructed and invested
with new powers.   It was entrusted with the powers
of parliament in the intervals between the sessions.
Thus it had political, legislative, and judicial functions,
and it wielded its new authority with an imperious
hand.   The Court of Session was reconstituted to
supersede the courts which Cromwell had introduced.

Acting on the king's instructions the privy council
proclaimed the reintroduction of Episcopacy in September, 1661 ; and the scramble for the bishoprics
immediately began.   James Sharp had secured the
primacy for himself ; and the other bishops selected
by the Court were men of meagre abilities, poorly
qualified to command the respect and reverence
of the people.   But the king and the council enjoined the people to pay all due deference to the
archbishops and bishops.   Parliament passed Acts to
secure the new order, patronage was restored, and the
ministers were commanded to receive presentation
from their patrons and institution from their bishops.
The new hierarchy thrust upon the nation was a
curious establishment : it had no liturgy ; the whole
discipline of the Church·was placed in the hands of
the bishops ; and the bishops themselves were entirely
dependent on the king, who was made pope and
despot by the parliament of Scotland.

In the end of September, 1662, the royal commissioner and members of the privy council proceeded to
the west to enforce obedience to the bishops and the
new laws.   The Archbishop of Glasgow complained

that few of the ministers in his district had presented themselves for institution. On the 1st of October the council met in Glasgow, and passed an Act which announced that all the ministers who had not complied with the law should lose their livings, and commanded them to remove from their manses and parishes before the 1st of November, and not to reside within the bounds of their respective presbyteries. Three hundred of the ministers left their parishes rather than subject themselves to Episcopacy and political bondage. These presbyterian ministers and all who joined them were severely punished.

A contest arose between Middleton, the royal commissioner, and the Earl of Lauderdale, the secretary. In the spring of 1663, Middleton's commission was recalled, and the king dismissed him. The Earl of Rothes was appointed royal commissioner; but Lauderdale obtained and long held the ascendency in the government of Scotland.

Rothes and Lauderdale arrived in Edinburgh in June, 1663, and Parliament reassembled on the 18th. Another oppressive Act was passed to subdue all opposition to the bishops and the new curates. It reasserted that the king had determined to maintain the government of the Church by archbishops and bishops, "and not to endure nor give in to any variation in the least." The ejected ministers were prohibited from preaching or assuming any of their functions under the penalty of sedition. All persons were commanded to attend public worship in their own parish churches on Sunday; and, if absent, they incurred the following fines :—Each noble or land-

owner the sum of one-fourth of his annual rental;
each tenant a fourth of his movable goods; each
burgess a fourth of his movable goods and the loss
of his freedom of trading and all privileges in the
borough.   This Act was rigorously enforced.

Some of the ejected ministers still resided in their
parishes, and the people flocked to hear their preaching.   Thus the religious meetings arose which the
authorities called "Conventicles," meaning unlawful
or seditious meetings.   The privy council issued a
series of oppressive Acts against persons who attended
such meetings, or absented themselves from the
churches on Sunday.   Detachments of troops were
sent to the west, the south-west, and the south, to
execute the law upon all who withdrew from the
parish churches and exact the fines from all offenders.
The process of fining was summary.   The curate
accused whom he pleased to any one of the officers
of the army, who acted as judge; no witnesses were
required; and the soldiers executed the sentence.
Very often the fine far exceeded what the law
allowed.

The persecution continued with increasing severity.
At last the people, driven past the limits of human
endurance and goaded to desperation, turned on
their oppressors.   The first open act of resistance
occurred in the vicinity of the village of Dalry, in
Galloway, in November, 1666, when four countrymen
rescued an old man whom the soldiers were mal-
treating to extort his church fines.   They were soon
joined by others, and disarmed the small detachment
of soldiers quartered in the district.   Having com-

mitted themselves, they resolved to surprise Sir James Turner and marched on Dumfries. They entered the town on the morning of the 15th of November, took Sir James a prisoner, and disarmed his men.

They proceeded to Ayrshire, where they expected much support. But some of the leading men of the county were in prison, few joined their standard, and the enterprise seemed hopeless. The insurgents then marched into Lanark, and in that county their numbers reached two thousand men ; but they had no organisation or discipline. They renewed the Covenant and issued a manifesto. They advanced to the neighbourhood of Edinburgh, but were unable to take it, and retired southward to the Pentland Hills. On the 28th of November, Dalziel, with the royal army, came upon the insurgents ; and after a slight encounter completely defeated them. About fifty of the insurgents were slain, and one hundred taken prisoners.

The prisoners were taken to Edinburgh to be tried. Some of them were unmercifully tortured with the boot to extort a confession, but they had nothing to confess. Nineteen of them were hanged in Edinburgh, and some in Glasgow, Ayr, Irvine, and Dumfries ; altogether forty were executed. Military execution followed, Dalziel and Drummond were dispatched westward to crush the spirit of rebellion, and compel the people to embrace Episcopacy. The army acted with more rapacity than if it had been in an enemy's country, for everywhere the soldiers took free quarters. On the roads and in the fields they committed robbery and murder with impunity ; complaints only occasioned more suffering; suspicion was accepted as evidence of guilt; no proof of innocence was allowed or mitigating circumstance considered. Many acts of extreme cruelty and outrage have been recorded, but I forbear to detail these sickening scenes.

Much of the odium of the persecution was attributed to Archbishop Sharp, who was believed to have insisted on severe measures of repression. In 1668 the Government were showing some leniency to the Presbyterians, when James Mitchell, a young man concerned in the late rising, attempted to assassinate the archbishop. On the 11th of July, in Edinburgh, the archbishop came from his lodgings and stepped into his coach with the Bishop of Orkney, when a shot was discharged at him which missed him, but shattered the Bishop of Orkney's arm. Mitchell crossed the street and instantly disappeared; and he was not taken till six years afterwards. The Government raised a loud clamour about this attempt, offered a reward for the apprehension of the assassin, and renewed the outcry against the Presbyterians and their meetings.

In spite of the severe measures of the Government the field meetings of the disaffected people continued to increase. In 1678 a large army was posted chiefly in the south-western counties; and in the beginning of the following year detachments of troops were ordered to march up and down the country, to harass all who did not conform to Episcopacy, and to collect the taxes which many of the people would not pay till compelled. The soldiers were commanded to pursue all who attended field meetings, to kill all who resisted, and to imprison and deliver to the magistrates all whom they could apprehend. The existing resources of law being found inadequate, the king appointed an army of special sheriff deputies, expressly to try persons accused of attending field meetings, withdrawing from the parish churches, and irregular marriages and baptisms. That some of the men thus invested with special powers would act with an imperious hand was certain ; and when William Carmichael, an ex-bailie of Edinburgh, was raised to the dignity of a special sheriff in the county of Fife, of course he exerted himself to the utmost to show that he was worthy of his post. He treated the people who attended field meetings in Fife with great severity. A few bold men determined to frighten him. On the 3rd of May, 1679, a party under Hackston of Rathillet and John Balfour attempted to waylay him among the hills above Cupar, where they expected him to be hunting. They searched for him from early morning to past midday without success. But when they were going to disperse tidings came that the primate was in the neighbourhood, and would pass along the road in his coach. They now bethought that if the subordinate had escaped, providence had placed their great enemy within their grasp.

The archbishop's coach was driving along Magus Moor, about two miles from his own city, and the party instantly pursued it. Sharp cried to the coachman to drive hard, the pursuers fired shots, overtook the coach, cut the traces, disarmed and dismounted

his attendants, and commanded Judas to come forth,
that they might not injure his daughter who was in
the coach screaming with terror.   They dragged him
out, and he fell on his knees and in piteous tones
implored them to spare his life, promising them
forgiveness—anything if they would show mercy ; but
they reminded him that he had imbrued his hands
in the blood of many innocent people for a period of
eighteen years, and that now he must die.   A volley
of shot was discharged at him and his life was extinguished with their swords.   After rifling the coach
and the bishop's clothes, the assassins remounted and
rode off, leaving the primate's daughter lamenting
over his mangled body on the moor.

There were a few persons in Scotland who approved
of this foul deed, but the majority of the people
regarded it as an atrocious murder.   Assassination
and murder cannot be justified under any circumstances.

A reward was offered by the Government for the
apprehension of the murderers, but they fled to the
west where they were joined by others, and prepared
to resist the authorities.   A few of the most determined agreed to issue "a public Testimony against
the Government," and arranged to meet on the 29th
of May, the anniversary of the Restoration.   A party
of eighty armed men marched into the town of
Rutherglen, extinguished the bonfires blazing in
honour of the day, burned the Acts of Parliament
which established Episcopacy, read their declaration,
and affixed it to the market cross.

A great field meeting was to be held at Loudon

Hill, in Clydedale, on Sunday, the 7th of June, 1679 ; and Graham of Claverhouse, on hearing of their design, resolved to disperse them. The service of the day had begun when the watchmen observed a body of troopers approaching. Graham's dragoons appeared on the rising ground. Amongst the Covenanters there were such fighting men as Hackston, Balfour, and William Cleland, and the assemblage determined on battle. They advanced to a swampy piece of ground and took up their position. Graham attempted to charge, and after a sharp and short engagement he was completely defeated, and twenty of his troopers were slain. The event is known in history as Drumclog. Encouraged by this success the insurgents marched on Glasgow, but they were unable to take it, and retired to Hamilton and formed a camp. Many there joined them from Ayrshire, Galloway, and other parts of the kingdom ; and in a few days they numbered four thousand men. The extreme party of the Government had produced what they much desired—a general insurrection, which afforded them an occasion for insisting on the utmost persecution of the Presbyterians.

The Duke of Monmouth, the king's natural son, was commissioned to command the royal army and suppress the rebellion. He arrived in Edinburgh on the 18th of June, and placed himself at the head of the army. On the 21st he marched westward and came in sight of the insurgents lying on Hamilton Moor. The insurgents had little organisation or discipline, and their leaders disagreed and failed to

present a united front.   On the 22nd the royal army
advanced to the attack, the insurgents were utterly
defeated, many were slain in the flight, and more than
a thousand taken prisoners.   Still, in the words of
Hogg :—

> " When rank oppression rends the heart,
>   And rules wi' stroke o' death,
> Wha wadna spend their dear heart's blood,
>   For the tenets of their faith."

The engagement was called the battle of Bothwell
Bridge.

Next day the prisoners, tied two and two, were
driven into Edinburgh and placed in the Grayfriars
churchyard, and kept in the open air for weeks.   Two
of the insurgent ministers were hanged at the Grass
Market ; and five of the prisoners were executed on
Magus Moor as an atonement for the murder of the
primate.   Such of the prisoners as admitted that the
rising was a rebellion and promised submission, were
liberated ; but upward of two hundred, who declined
to accept these terms, were crammed into a ship and
transported to Barbadoes, to be sold as slaves in the
plantations.   The Government continued to persecute
all who attended field meetings and absented themselves from the parish churches.

In October, 1680, the Duke of York arrived in
Scotland.   With the aim of strengthening his pros-
pective claim to the throne Parliament was summoned
to meet at Edinburgh in July, 1681, and he assumed
the post of royal commissioner.   An Act was passed
touching the succession, which repeated the assertion

"that the kings of the realm derived their royal
power from God alone," and succeeded to it by lineal
descent, which could not be altered without involving
the nation in perjury and rebellion. That no difference in religion, law, or Act of Parliament, could
divert the right of succession to the Crown from the

THE MAIDEN.

nearest heir ; and all who opposed this incurred the
penalties of high treason. A new Test Act was passed,
which contained such a jumble of inconsistencies that
many declined to sign it. The Earl of Argyle proposed to take it in so far as it was consistent, and

16

stated that he could not bind himself from doing what was incumbent as a loyal subject. For this he was charged with high treason, tried, and convicted; but he escaped from the castle of Edinburgh and fled to Holland.

During the years of 1682, '83, and '84, the troops continued to harass and persecute the people. The soldiers pillaged farmhouses, exacted free quarters, levied enormous fines, and seized and imprisoned all who were refractory. Many of the Covenanters were shot down without trial; and the nation groaned under the yoke of dire oppression. Still, in spite of the savage persecution, the remnant of the Covenanters stood unshaken and untouched in their principles and faith, proclaiming war against the Government and the king. Who can blame them? Whether was it best for the peace and civilisation of the island that an absolute king should reign in undisputed power over everything, or that a measure of liberty and freedom of opinion should be allowed to the people? This in some form had become the problem which then filled all thoughtful minds in Britain.

The year 1685 opened in Scotland amid the gloom of persecution. No one was safe from the violence of the army; many were shot on the highways, in the fields and mountains, and at their own doors. And the reign of Charles II. closed on the 6th of February amidst a scene of oppression, suffering, and corruption, unmatched in the worst times of the nation's history.

The Duke of York now mounted the throne, and on the 10th of February, he was proclaimed as "the only, the undoubted, and lawful king of the realm."

James VII. dispensed with the coronation oath, lest it should seem that he in any way derived his right and power from the people. Parliament assembled at Edinburgh on the 23rd of April, and proceeded to legislate in accordance with the views of the new king. New and severer Acts were passed to exterminate the Covenanters. It was enacted that all who attended field meetings incurred the penalty of death. Husbands were made responsible for the attendance of their wives at church and liable for their fines ; and the Test Act was renewed with additions.

The Earl of Argyle had entered into the plans of the exiles in Holland, and in concert with the Duke of Monmouth, concocted an invasion of Britain. Argyle landed in Scotland in May, 1685, but his attempt utterly failed. He was captured on the 18th of June, and carried to Edinburgh. The king and the council determined to execute him according to the terms of his former sentence, and he was beheaded on the 30th of June. The people expressed much sympathy for him, and looked on his execution as a cruel murder.

This unsuccessful attempt against the Government only increased the number of sufferers. The prisons were crowded with people incarcerated for nonconformity and rebellion, and huddled together without distinction of sex in the most wretched condition. In September upwards of one hundred of these prisoners were shipped for New Jersey. But on the passage fever broke out, and when they reached the New World only forty of them were alive. Fortunately the magistrates of New Jersey declared that they were free men, and in a foreign land they enjoyed the liberty which had been ruthlessly denied to them at home.

In the winter of 1686, James VII. advanced his scheme for the reintroduction of Roman Catholicism. He proposed that all should have liberty of conscience, and expatiated on the blessing which would result from a universal toleration of religious opinions. He asked the Scotch Parliament to give toleration and equal rights to Roman Catholics, but this was not granted. James then issued a proclamation in the following terms :—" We by our sovereign authority, royal prerogative, and absolute power, which all our subjects are to obey without reserve, do hereby give and grant our royal toleration to the several professors of the Christian religion, under the conditions hereafter mentioned. We tolerate the moderate Presbyterians to meet in their private houses. . . . . Meantime it is our royal-pleasure that field meetings and such as preach at them or attend them, shall be prosecuted to the utmost severity of the laws against them, seeing that from these rendezvous of rebellion so much disorder has proceeded, and so much disturbance to the Government. . . . In like manner we hereby tolerate Quakers. . . . And, considering the severe and cruel laws made against the Roman Catholics, ... we with advice of our privy council, by our sovereign authority and absolute power, suspend, stop, and make void, all laws and Acts of Parliament, or constitutions, against Roman Catholics, so that they shall in all things be as free as any of our

Protestant subjects, not only to exercise their religion, but also to enjoy all places and other posts which we shall think fit to bestow upon them." Amen.

On the 5th of July, James suspended all the penal laws against nonconformity. Many of the Presby-terian ministers were released from prison, and others who 'had been banished soon returned home. But the real Covenanters quickly recognised the meaning of the king's toleration. What right had he to forbid or to allow them to preach the gospel ? They had a warrant from a higher Master ; and therefore they continued their field meetings, scorning alike his claim of absolute power and his denunciations against them. Their leader and preacher, Renwick, was seized in February, 1688, and executed at Edinburgh ; and his death terminated the religious executions in Scotland.

The crisis had been long preparing, and when it was seen to be nigh, great excitement arose in Scot-land. As the convictions and sentiment of the people had been long repressed, the rebound threatened to be violent. Although attempts were made to sup-press the Prince of Orange's declaration, which was issued in the middle of October, 1688, its import soon became known in Scotland. All the forces in the kingdom were called away by the king to operate against the Dutch, who had landed in England. When the Scotch bishops saw the dark clouds gather-ing, they assembled at Edinburgh on the 3rd of November, and resolved to despatch a letter to the king, in which they prayed—" That God in His mercy, who has so often preserved and delivered your

Majesty, will still preserve and deliver you, by giving you the hearts of your subjects, and the necks of your enemies."

Before the issue of the military operations in England was decided, disturbances arose in Edinburgh. The Earl of Perth, Chancellor and head of the privy council, had been very servile to the king, and therefore an object of hatred, but now his courage failed and he fled to his country residence. When it became clear that the king's cause was falling, excited crowds gathered on the streets of Edinburgh and shouted for a free parliament. On Sunday, the 9th of December, a number of students, apprentices, and others, appeared on the streets, proceeded to the market cross, and proclaimed a reward of four hundred pounds sterling to any one who should seize the Earl of Perth, and bring him there dead or alive.

All kinds of rumours were rife. A report spread that an army of Irish Catholics were on the eve of landing in Galloway, and the people dreaded a massacre. As the army had been sent into England and the Government had dissolved, there was a collapse of authority. The people in the western counties assembled in crowds, and took the law into their own hands. They naturally resolved to purge the Church, and began on the 25th of December. Some of the obnoxious curates had saved themselves by flight, and those who remained were rudely turned out of their manses, ordered to depart and never return to the parishes. Upwards of two hundred of the curates were thus removed.

Some of the Scotch nobles were in London when

the Prince of Orange arrived, and many others hastened there to offer him their service. On the 7th of January, 1689, he requested them to meet him at Whitehall. The meeting was led by the Duke of Hamilton, and numbered upwards of one hundred men of note. The prince desired them to delibe-rate and inform him how he could promote the peace and interest of their country. After debating three days, they agreed to resolutions embodied in an address to the prince, requesting him to summon a parliament to meet at Edinburgh on the 14th of March, and to assume the government of the king-dom. To this he at once acceded.

Preparations for the elections were immediately commenced, all parties being anxious to return mem-bers to decide the future position of the nation. The prince assumed the power to dispense with a number of restrictions, and ordered that the members of the boroughs should be elected by a poll of all the adult inhabitants. His supporters secured a majority of members ; while King James's party mainly relied on the support of the Duke of Gordon, who commanded the castle of Edinburgh, and on the Viscount Dundee, whose energy was well known and greatly feared.

The Convention assembled at the appointed time. Forty-two peers, forty-nine members for the counties, fifty for the boroughs, and nine bishops, constituted the assemblage. The election of a president was the first business. The supporters of James proposed the Marquis of Athole ; the Whigs (William's supporters) proposed the Duke of Hamilton, and he was elected

by a majority of forty.   On the 16th of March a
letter from William was read, which expressed his
desire that the Convention should settle the religion
and liberties of the kingdom in accordance with the
convictions of the people and the public good.   The
same day a letter from King James was read, but it
was not calculated to inspire hope in his cause.   He
offered pardon to those who immediately returned to
their allegiance, to others no mercy could be granted.
His adherents in the Convention were mortified, his
enemies vehement, and the sitting closed in a scene of
excitement.

The citizens of Edinburgh were intensely agitated
as well as the members of the Convention.   As the
Duke of Gordon had refused to surrender the castle
of Edinburgh, it was known that the Jacobites would
not yield without a severe struggle, and at any
moment they might attempt some desperate move.
When the Convention met on the 18th, tidings were
brought into the House that Viscount Dundee was
on the Stirling road with a troop of dragoons, and
that he was seen conferring with the Duke of Gordon
at the castle gate.   This news threw the members
into a state of violent alarm, and Hamilton, the president, started to his feet and cried : " It is high time
that we should look to ourselves. The enemies of our
religion and of our civil freedom are mustering all
around us, and we may well suspect that they have
accomplices even here.   Lock the doors !   Lay the
keys on the table !   Let no one go out but those
lords and gentlemen, whom we shall appoint to call
the citizens to arms !   There are some good men from

the west in Edinburgh, men for whom I can answer."
The majority of the members shouted assent, and
what he proposed was immediately done. The Earl
of Leven went out and ordered the drums to be beat,
and the Covenanters promptly answered to the call
and mustered in such force as overawed all the
Jacobites in Edinburgh. They protected the Convention till the arrival of the Scotch regiments under
General Mackay.

The Convention prepared to settle the prime point
of the conflict. As usual a committee was appointed,
consisting of eight peers, eight representatives of the
boroughs, and eight of the counties. They proceeded to debate and frame the decisive resolution,
which finally assumed the following form : " That
James VII. had assumed the royal power and acted
as king without ever taking the oath required by law;
and by the advice of evil counsellors he had invaded
the fundamental constitution of the kingdom, and
altered it from a limited monarchy to an arbitrary
and despotic power, and did exercise the same to the
subversion of the Protestant religion, and the violation
of the laws and the liberties of the kingdom ; whereby
he forfeited his right to the Crown, and his throne has
become vacant." This resolution was accompanied
by another, which tendered the Crown to William and
Mary ; and both were carried, only three members and
seven bishops voting against them. Immediately
after the new sovereigns were proclaimed at the cross
of Edinburgh.

The Convention also framed and adopted a Claim of
Right, which was presented with the resolutions tender-

ing the Crown.   It was intended to indicate the law
as it then stood, and also to show what constitutions
and liberties the late kings had infringed and violated.
The chief points of this important claim were these :
That all proclamations assuming an absolute power
to suspend the laws were illegal ; that the measures
employed to establish popery, the imposing of bonds
and oaths, and the exacting of money from the nation
without the authority of parliament were contrary to
law.   That it was illegal to invest the officers of the
army with judicial powers to inflict death without
trial, jury, or record ;· to imprison persons without
expressing the reason why, or to delay their trial ; to
prosecute and procure the forfeiture of persons by
straining obsolete statutes ; to nominate the magistrates and common council of the boroughs ; to dictate
the proceedings in courts of justice ; to use torture
without evidence or in ordinary crimes ; to garrison
private houses, or to introduce a hostile army into the
country to live at free quarters in a time of peace.
That prelacy or the superiority of any office in the
church above presbyters is, and has been, a great and
insufferable grievance and trouble to the nation, ever
since the Reformation, when they were reformed from
popery to presbytery ; and therefore prelacy ought to
be abolished.   The right of appeal to parliament, and
of petition to the throne, were reaffirmed ; frequent
meetings of parliament were demanded ; and all the
preceding points were declared to be undoubted rights,
against which no proclamation or precedent ought to
operate to the injury of the people.

XVI.

THE REVOLUTION AND THE UNION.

ALTHOUGH at the centre of authority the Revolution had been accomplished, the difficulties and problems which had caused it were not solved. The opposite interests, the diverse convictions and sentiments in religion and politics, which had characterised parties in Scotland since the Reformation, were not harmonised. The deposed dynasty had still many adherents in Scotland, and the new government found itself face to face with a complicated series of obstacles. The Covenanters were dissatisfied with the way in which the Convention had approached the question of Church government ; the bishops and Episcopal party were bitterly offended and disappointed ; and the leading Jacobites were preparing to assail the new government by force of arms.

King William had a difficult task in nominating ministers for the government of Scotland. As the leaders of a revolutionary movement always imagine that each of them is supremely entitled to an important post in the new arrangement of affairs, hence, whomsoever the king might appoint, he would offend those who found their own claims ignored. Numbers of Scotsmen were eager to proffer their advice and service to King William; and his position as King of Scotland was perplexing inasmuch as both the Church and Parliament demanded reform of a radical character. But there was one Scotsman whom the king could trust, William Carstairs, a Presbyterian minister, afterwards Principal of the University of Edinburgh. He had suffered persecution under the preceding reigns, and his hand still bore the marks of the thumbscrew. William of Orange knew him and implicitly trusted him, and no man of that period was more worthy of confidence. He was appointed Chaplain to their Majesties for Scotland. But he continued to be much with the king, and advised him to adopt a moderate policy in Scotland. Carstairs' own sentiments were liberal, and the severe persecution which he had undergone had not in the least hardened his nature or clouded the judgment of his remarkable mind.

When the Convention was turned into a parliament, the Duke of Hamilton appeared as Royal Commissioner; the Earl of Crawford was nominated President of Parliament; Lord Melville, who commanded the confidence of the Presbyterians, was appointed Secretary of State. Sir James Montgomery considered himself entitled to the secretaryship, and although he was offered the office of Lord Justice Clerk, he thought it below his merits, and returned from London to Edinburgh a disappointed man, full of feelings of aversion to the king, and determined to concert plans of opposition to the Government. He soon gathered around him a number of kindred spirits, the Earl of Annandale, Lord Ross, and others, and organised a formal and bold opposition, which was a novel feature in a Scotch Parliament.

The Convention reassembled on the 15th of June, 1689, and was turned into a parliament. Much of the session was spent in fruitless efforts. But an Act abolishing Episcopacy was passed. The castle of Edinburgh surrendered on the 14th of June, the Duke of Gordon and the garrison receiving an indemnity, and marching out with arms and baggage.

Meanwhile Viscount Dundee and the Jacobites in the north were struggling to the utmost against the Government. Since Dundee left Edinburgh, he had concerted a rising in the Highlands. General Mackay with the royal army was making desperate but unavailing efforts to crush the rising. His first campaign in the Highlands was an utter failure. Dundee resolved to muster the chiefs and clansmen in Lochaber, and a force of about two thousand assembled. He marched through Badenoch to Athole, and arrived at Blair Castle on the morning of the 27th of July, 1689, when he received tidings that the royal army under Mackay had entered the Pass of Killiecrankie. Dundee allowed Mackay to advance through the Pass, and gave him battle on the open ground. He marched from the castle of Blair along the Water of Tilt, and turned round the Hill of Lude, and took up his position on the brow of the hill which overlooked Mackay's army. When Mackay perceived the approach of Dundee's followers, he prepared for action.

His army consisted of 3,500 men, and two troops of cavalry. He formed his men in one line three deep. Near the centre of his line was a piece of marshy ground, and behind it he placed his cavalry, which might be ready to attack the enemy in flank, after the fire of the line was spent. His line of battle was longer than Dundee's, hence, when the latter was advancing to the attack, some companies of the clansmen were exposed to a raking flank fire. The two armies faced each other for several hours, and the Highlanders were becoming impatient. At three quarters of an hour before sunset they were ordered to prepare for action, and Dundee placed himself at the head of his cavalry and resolved to charge in person. The signal to charge was given, and the clansmen raised a shout which re-echoed afar from the surrounding hills. They advanced down the hill firing their guns, but the royal line returned the fire briskly, and thinned their ranks. As they came close upon the hostile line, they threw down their guns, drew their broadswords, and, with yells, rushed on the royalists before these had time to fix their bayonets. The onset was fierce and irresistible, and at once broke the ranks of the enemy, who had no effective means of defence against the strokes of the broadswords, and the royal troops fled down the valley in utter confusion. In a few minutes the battle of Killiecrankie was fought and won. Dundee fell mortally wounded by a shot, and expired in the moment of victory; and about six hundred of his followers were slain.

In spite of the disaster, General Mackay never lost

his coolness and courage. As soon as he saw Dundee's mode of attack, he ordered his cavalry to charge the clansmen in flank. In person he led a troop to charge their right flank, and spurred through the thickest of the enemy, but only one single horseman followed their general. When he turned round to observe the state of matters, his army was out of sight ; "in the twinkling of an eye," he said, " our men were out of sight, having gone down pell mell to the river, where the baggage stood." After some time, he found that only about four hundred of his army remained ; some of his men had fled, and two thousand of them were slain or taken prisoners. Having collected the remnants of his army, he placed himself at its head, and retired from the scene of the battle. His officers recommended a retreat through the Pass of Killiecrankie, but he wisely rejected their advice, and proceeded across the hills toward Strath Tay, and thence to Stirling, which he reached on the 29th of July.

News of the defeat of the royal army reached Edinburgh on the 28th of July, the day after the battle, and caused intense consternation. It was reported that Mackay was killed and his army destroyed ; that Dundee was already master of the country beyond the Forth, and rapidly advancing to take possession of the capital. A meeting of the Privy Council was immediately held, and orders issued to muster all the fencible men in the west, and to concentrate all the troops at Stirling to defend the passage of the Forth. Some of the members of the Council proposed to transfer the seat of government to Glasgow, others were for retiring into England. This ferment continued for two days, but on the third intelligence was received of Dundee's death—an event which was regarded both in Edinburgh and London as a full compensation for the defeat and destruction of the royal army. The fall of Dundee was a fatal blow to the cause of King James in Scotland. Cannon, who succeeded him in command, mismanaged everything; the war languished, and soon ceased.

In 1690, Parliament sanctioned the Westminster Confession of Faith, and re-established the Presbyterian polity. The re-organisation of the Church was entrusted to the ministers ejected in 1662, sixty of whom still survived, and such ministers and elders as they thought fit to associate with themselves in the work. Patronage was abolished, and the nomination of ministers entrusted to the heritors and elders of the parish. The meetings of the General Assemblies, Synods, and Presbyteries, were resumed, and the work of moral teaching and education proceeded.

Though open war against the Government had ceased, the exiled king had many adherents in the north and among the Highland chiefs. And therefore an attempt was made to purchase their friendship. The king and his Government avowedly adopted a scheme of bribery and corruption. It must be told that if morality and truth be the standard of estimation, William III. and his advisers have little claim to be regarded as examples of humanity.

The Government engaged the Earl of Breadalbane to purchase the submission of the Highland chiefs and secure their allegiance to William III. A sum of twenty thousand pounds was placed at his disposal.

He was instructed to pay particular attention to Sir Donald McDonald, Maclean, Clanronald, Glengarry, Lochiel, and the Mackenzies. The chiefs were suspicious of Breadalbane, and little progress was made. A proclamation was issued in August, 1691, which commanded all the Highland chiefs to take the oath of allegiance in the presence of a magistrate before the 1st of January, 1692, under the penalties of treason and military execution. Most of the chiefs did at the last comply with the terms of the proclamation.

But some of the king's advisers, and one man in particular, were greatly disappointed that the Highland chiefs were yielding to the demands of the Government. Sir John Dalrymple of Stair, the Secretary of State for Scotland, was extremely anxious that a number of the chiefs should stand out and afford an excuse for their complete extermination. There is ample evidence that he became wildly angry as his hope of a great slaughter of the Celtic people day by day appeared less probable. His letters show that he was grasping to the utmost to attain this result. In October, 1691, he wrote—" It must be a strange inadventure if the Highlanders be not convinced of the king's extraordinary goodness to them, when he is content to be at a charge to accommodate them, and give them the plain prospect of future peace, security, and advantage, when he can gratify many by destroying them with as little charge. And certainly, if there do remain any obstinacy, these advices will be taken. The king, by his offer of mercy, has sufficiently shown his good intentions, and by their ruin he will rid himself of a suspicious crew." In November, he intimated to Breadalbane — "I wrote to you formerly, that if the rest were willing to concur, as the crows do, to pull down Glengarry's nest this winter, so as the king be not hindered to draw four regiments from Scotland,—in that case destroying him and his clan . . . will be fully as acceptable as if he had come in. This answer all ends, and satisfies those who complain of the king's too great gentleness." On the eve of the massacre he wrote to the commander of the forces—"I assure you your power shall be full enough, and I hope the soldiers will not trouble the Government with prisoners." Again, "Just now, my Lord Argyle tells me that Glencoe has not taken the oaths, at which I rejoice ; it is a great work of charity to be exact in rooting out that damnable sept, the worst in all the Highlands."

Macdonald of Glencoe, owing to several untoward circumstances, was a few days behind the prescribed time for taking the oath of allegiance ; but he did take it before the Sheriff of Argyle at Inverary. And the sheriff forwarded it to the Privy Council in Edinburgh, but the clerks refused to take it. The upshot was that the massacre of the Chief of Glencoe and all his retainers was ordered by the king, and despatches sent to the commander of the forces in that quarter to execute it. On a cold stormy night, on the 13th of February, 1692, the chief and forty of his clan were murdered by the king's troops. But a number of the intended victims escaped, owing to the darkness of the night and the severity of the snowstorm, and fled almost naked to the rocks and mountains. The deserted houses of the doomed clan were burned down. The soldiers collected the property of their victims, which consisted of nine hundred cattle and two hundred ponies, and a number of sheep and goats, and drove the whole to Fort William, where they were divided among the officers of the garrison.

Although the massacre was deliberately planned and treacherously executed, it was not so complete as intended, for the storm prevented four hundred of the troops from reaching the scene till after the appointed hour. Politically it was a hideous blunder, as it tended to render the clans more suspicious, and roused in their hearts a bitter hatred of the Government. Attempts have been made to free the king of the responsibility of the massacre, though he not only authorised it, but by his subsequent action fully condoned it, and it has left a stain on his character which time has not obliterated.

The Government was much surprised at the sentiments of the people touching the massacre. Secretary Stair was greatly astonished when he heard the expressions in which he was characterised, and his faithful service to the king so bitterly assailed ; but he openly declared that his only regret was, that every soul of the clan was not slain on that stormy morning.

The efforts to extend the elements of education after the Reformation have already been mentioned. The Church, the local authorities, and the legislature, had continued in their endeavour to promote the work. In 1616, the Privy Council enacted that there should be a school in every parish of the kingdom. This was not

THE PASS OF GLENCOE.

fully carried out ; and ten years later they ordered a report on the state of the parishes throughout the kingdom, from which it appears that the majority of the parishes were then without regular schools. In 1633, Parliament ratified the act of the council, and empowered the bishops, with the consent of a majority of the parishioners, to impose a rate on the possessors of land, for establishing and supporting the parish schools. In 1641, the subject was again before Parliament ; and once more in 1645, when it was enacted, "that there should be a school founded, and a schoolmaster appointed in every parish, not already provided." For this purpose a rate was to be imposed, and a scheme of the modification of the tax drawn out ; but troubles came fast and thick upon the party then at the head of affairs, and this Act was not put into operation.

In 1696, Parliament enacted that there should be a school and schoolmaster established in every parish, not already provided, "by the advice of the pro- prietors and ministers of the parish." This Act is definite and clearly drawn. It made provisions for imposing a rate on the owners of land to erect and maintain school buildings, and pay the schoolmasters' salaries. From this date the parish system of primary schools became established, and continued without interruption, excepting in some parts of the Highlands, where the parishes were so large as to render the Act inoperative ; but ultimately other means of providing elementary education in those remote parts of the kingdom were adopted.

Throughout this period there were elementary

schools in many of the towns, distinct from the grammar schools.   But it should be observed that the grammar schools, from an early period enjoyed a monopoly of teaching certain branches, being protected more or less strictly until recent times. Education, like trade and everything else, was subject to the spirit and influence of the age.

After the Revolution the spirit of the nation began to incline more to industry, to the erection of manufactories, to trade, and to commerce.   Dreams of vast wealth rose before the national imagination, and captivated it ; and a man appeared with dazzling schemes to meet the cravings of the people.   William Paterson's mind overflowed with grand commercial projects.   As a part of the Isthmus of Darien was unoccupied by the Spaniards, he formed the idea of founding on it a central emporium for the merchandise of the world.   He thought that a link could be formed there to connect the trade of Europe and Asia, so that the Atlantic and Pacific Oceans might be ploughed by ships from every quarter of the globe, directing their prows to this narrow neck of land, and thus enriching the Scots who would hold the keys of the commercial world in their hands.   The scheme assumed form in an Act of Parliament passed in 1695, which authorised the establishment of a trading company to America, Africa, and the Indies.

The company proposed a subscribed capital of £600,000.   When the books were opened in London, the £300,000 offered to the English merchants was quickly subscribed.   But the enterprise aroused the jealousy of the privileged English companies.

The House of Commons presented an address to the king against it, and seized the books and documents of the company. They concluded that the directors of the company were guilty of a high crime for attempting such a thing, and proposed to impeach them. These hostile proceedings alarmed the London subscribers, and they slipped out of the company by failing to pay the calls on their shares. This action of the English Government rather irritated than discouraged the Scots, and they pushed on their enterprise. Four weeks after the denunciations of the English Parliament, the subscription books were opened in Edinburgh, and on the first day £50,000 was subscribed, and within five months £400,000 was promised in Scotland.

The company proceeded with remarkable energy. They purchased six vessels from the Dutch and equipped them. On the 26th of July, 1698, three of their ships with twelve hundred men on board, sailed from Leith ; and on the 4th of November, they landed at a point on the Gulf of Darien. They built a fort to command the gulf, and marked two sites for towns, which they proposed to name New Edinburgh and New St. Andrews. They purchased the land which they occupied, from the natives, and sent friendly messages to all the Spanish Governors within their reach. They proclaimed freedom of trade and toleration of religion to all nations.

But their privations soon began, and the causes of the failure of the undertaking are easily understood. There was a lack of experience and trading skill among them ; they had no definite political organisation ; and there was no adequate provision made for sending instructions and assistance to them from home — a lamentable want of foresight. From their arrival till June of the following year, they received no communication from Scotland. There was no market for the merchandise which they had taken with them. By and by, they began to feel the sad pressure of want, and the continued effects of insufficient food and pestilence rapidly reduced their numbers. The disheartening task of burying their dead soon arrested their energy ; and when spring came, nothing but certain death awaited them, if they remained. Accordingly they resolved to leave the settlement, and within eight months from the time they landed, they evacuated it. They placed themselves in the ships, which, owing to the number of the sick, were imperfectly manned. They sailed in June, 1699, and two of their ships arrived at New York in August, but those alive were almost exhausted, and few of them survived.

At the time when the colonists were leaving the settlement, the company was fitting out other expeditions. Two ships sailed in May, with provisions, and stores ; and in September, another expedition followed, consisting of 1,300 men. On arriving they found the fort and huts destroyed, and the chief indication of their countrymen was their numerous graves. Shortly after landing, they discovered that the Spaniards were preparing to attack them. After one successful military effort, in which a small body of the Scots attacked and defeated a portion of the Spanish army, they were besieged by sea and land. In March, 1700, they surrendered to the Spaniards. Few of them ever returned to their native land.

When definite tidings of the final evacuation of the Darien settlement arrived, the nation rose to a height of frenzy rarely manifested. The Jacobites were wroth, and exerted themselves to the utmost to fan the flame of the national indignation, as a weapon of opposition to the king and the Government. The national pride of the Scots was deeply wounded ; and they strongly asserted that the failure of the colony was caused by the action of the king and the English Government.

Addresses were sent to the king, but he declined to receive them, and the indignation continued. The Scotch Parliament was soon overwhelmed with addresses and petitions from all ranks, and every quarter of the kingdom. The majority of the House warmly supported the petitions, and moved resolutions, which condemned the interference of the English Government in the Darien colony. After long and vehement debates, the final address to the king was carried by one hundred votes to sixty, on the 17th of January, 1701. It is a well-drawn and able paper—a complete vindication of the company, containing four resolutions : 1. Condemning the proceedings of the English Parliament with regard to the company, as an undue interference in the affairs of Scotland, " and an invasion upon the sovereignty and independence of our king and Parliament." 2. Declaring that the action of the English Envoy at Luxemburg was injurious to the interest of the company, " contrary to the law of nations and an

open encroachment upon the sovereignty and independence of this Crown and kingdom." 3. Con-.
demning the action and the proclamations of the
English Colonies against the Darien colony. 4.
Declaring that although the settlement of Darien
was formed in conformity with the company's Act
of Parliament, the Spaniards had treated the colonists as enemies and pirates ; and "that our Indian
and African Company's Colony of Caledonia in
Darien, in the Continent of America, was, and is,
legal and rightful."

The relations between the two kingdoms became
strained to the utmost.   And the king saw that the
only way of maintaining peace in Scotland was a
union of the two nations.   On the 28th of February,
1701, he reminded the English Parliament of his
proposal touching the union of England and Scotland.
But he died on the 8th of March, 1702.

Queen Anne's accession was hailed with applause
in Scotland. The Revolution Parliament re-assembled
at Edinburgh on the 19th of June, 1702.   It passed
resolutions touching Darien, and appointed commissioners to treat of a Union between the two
kingdoms.   The English Parliament authorised
commissioners to treat of the Union.   The commissioners of both nations met on the 10th of
November, and held many meetings ; but they could
not agree on the trading privileges, the English being
extremely loth to concede equal trading rights to the
Scots.

In the spring of 1703, Scotland was agitated by
the elections for the New Parliament summoned by

the Queen. The Jacobites struggled to the utmost, and succeeded in returning a considerable number of their party. The new House met on the 10th of May, the Duke of Queensberry appeared as royal commissioner, and the business of this memorable parliament began. All the laws in favour of Presbyterianism were ratified ; it was declared to be treason to speak against the " Claim of Right ; " and the Earl of Strathmore proposed an Act of toleration. One Act affirmed that the sovereign had no right to make war without the consent of the Scotch Parliament ; and another removed the restrictions upon the importation of French wines. Some proposals of a republican character were mooted, and Fletcher proposed to take the patronage of offices from the Crown and place it in the hands of Parliament.

On the Act for the security of the kingdom there was a long and warm debate, but it was carried. It enacted that on the demise of the queen without issue, the Scotch Parliament would appoint a successor from the Protestant descendants of the royal line of Scotland ; but the recognised successor to the throne of England was directly excluded, unless such conditions of government were settled as would secure the honour and sovereignty of the kingdom, and free religion and the trade of the nation from English influence. The coronation oath was not to be administered without instructions from Parliament under the penalty of treason. Another clause commanded that the nation should be placed in a state of defence, and all the able-bodied men immediately

mustered under their usual leaders.   The royal assent
was refused to this Act, and a storm of denunciation
was thus raised against the English.   Some of the
members now talked of rather dying like freemen
than living as slaves ; and when attempts were made
to stem their passions, they retorted that if denied
the freedom of expressing their opinions in Parliament,
they would proclaim them with their swords.

   This fierce antagonism between the two kingdoms
could not endure, and in spite of all obstacles the
Union was approaching.   Parliament re-assembled on
the 6th of July, 1704, the Marquis of Tweeddale took
his seat as royal commissioner, and the queen's
letter touched on the gravity of the situation.   She
appealed to Parliament to settle the succession ; but
they directly resolved not to name a successor to
the Crown till a satisfactory treaty with England for
the regulation of trade was concluded, and adopted
measures to secure the independence of the kingdom.
The Act of security was again passed and received the
royal assent.   Under it the Scots began to arm and
once more prepared to give battle to their enemy,
if he finally refused to accede to reasonable demands.

   The English Parliament met in 1705, and authorised a Treaty of Union to be negotiated between
England and Scotland.   The Crown was empowered
to appoint commissioners ; to meet and treat with any
body of commissioners authorised by the Scotch
Parliament ; and to place the result of their proceedings before the queen and the parliaments of
both kingdoms.

   On the 28th of June, the Scotch Parliament

assembled at Edinburgh, and the proposal of the English Government for a Union was the chief matter before it. There was a change in the ministry, and the Duke of Argyle appeared as royal commissioner. He was considered the most likely man to promote the important measure which had become necessary for the peace and civilisation of the island. The measure was surrounded with many difficulties; for the Jacobites were a strong party and determined to oppose the Union at every step, and if possible to defeat all attempts to settle the succession on the Revolution principles. The majority of Parliament resolved to hold to the demands for free trade and equal colonial rights; but some of the leading men among them were bitterly opposed to the incorporating provisions of the treaty.

A draft of the Act and commission for the treaty with England was read in Parliament on the 13th of July; and it was again brought before the House on the 25th of August. A long and hot debate ensued, and several amendments were proposed. But the Act was carried on the 1st of September, authorising the appointment of commissioners, the Duke of Athole with a number of followers protesting. The same day the question of the nomination of the commissioners was brought up—Were they to be appointed by Parliament or by the queen? The Duke of Hamilton moved that the nomination should be left to the queen; Fletcher of Saltoun bitterly opposed this, and the Jacobites supported him with all their might. After a warm debate Hamilton's motion was carried by a majority of forty, Athole again protesting, and the Jacobites adhering to him. The Jacobites were greatly enraged at this vote, and Lockhart, one of their most accomplished leaders, expressed his opinion of it in these words :—

"From this day we date the commencement of Scotland's ruin; and any person who will be at the trouble to reflect upon the management of this affair must be the more enraged when he sees how easily it might have been, and yet was not, prevented. For if the first restricting clause (which was lost by the unaccountable neglect of some members) had been carried, we should not have had one word more of the treaty; or had the nomination been left to the Parliament, those of the commissioners that represented the barons would have been so well chosen, that they might easily have obstructed the treaty from being brought to such a conclusion as afterwards happened."

It must be said, that on the Scotch side the queen or her advisers exercised a rare discretion in naming the list of commissioners. A well-considered effort was made to represent the different parties of the nation. Even the Jacobites were represented by one of their ablest men, Sir George Lockhart of Carnwath; though, by the desire of his party, he sat a silent member of the commission, and neither assented to anything nor made any protest.

The Union Commissioners, who were thirty-one on each side, met at Whitehall on the 16th of April, 1706. There had before been many attempts to form a Union of the two kingdoms, but this time the commissioners were in earnest and prepared to make every reasonable concession for the mutual advantage of both nations. They proceeded methodically, and approached the subject before them step by step, from both sides by turns in regular order, and finished their arduous undertaking in three months. According to the terms of the commission a copy of the treaty was presented to the queen, and her Majesty said :—

" My lords, I give you thanks for the great pains you have taken in this treaty, and am very well pleased to find that your endeavours have brought it to so good a conclusion. The particulars of it seem so reasonable, that I hope they will meet with approbation in the Parliaments of both kingdoms. I wish, therefore, that my servants of Scotland may lose no time in going down to propose it to my subjects of that kingdom ; and I shall always look upon it as a particular happiness, if this Union, which will be so great a security and advantage to both kingdoms, can be accomplished in my reign.'

The Scotch Parliament was therefore assembled on the 3rd of October, 1706. The Earl of Queensberry was appointed royal commissioner, and the Earl of Mar Secretary of State. Mar was well informed as to the designs of the Jacobites. At the first sitting the treaty was read and ordered to be printed, and circulated among the members. The minutes of the Union commissioners were also ordered to be printed.

A great and sustained effort was made in many parts of the kingdom to arouse popular feeling against the Union. Many pamphlets, papers, and ballads, were published and circulated throughout the country, which appealed to every prejudice and passion that was likely to rouse the wrath of the populace. Those who were proud of their ancestors and of national glory, were emphatically told that the ancient renown and independence of the kingdom were to be extinguished for ever. Many generations of Scotsmen had fought and struggled for their rights and liberties, endured hardship, persecution, and every form of privation; but now the degenerate sons of such a brave and noble race were about to barter away their glorious inheritance.

Though the outside pressure against the Union was strong and bitter, the Government was prepared to meet it. The Church threw her influence on the side of the Government. Still it seemed that the mass of popular feeling was with the opposition, and Parliament proceeded with its arduous work amid threatening circumstances.

On the 12th of October, the articles of the treaty were read one by one, and then discussed at the sittings from the 12th to the 30th of the month, suggestions being made from time to time, but no divisions taken. The first real effort of the opposition was made on the 4th of November, when it was moved that a vote should be taken on the first article of the Treaty of Union. A long debate ensued. The Duke of Hamilton delivered an animated speech on Scotch nationality. Seton of Pitmedden spoke in favour of the Union in a calm and well-reasoned address. But the great speech of the night was Lord Belhaven's.

LORD BELHAVEN.

It was a torrent of fierce rhetoric delivered with vehemence against the Union. It produced little impression on the members, but it was intended more for the outside public than for them, and was widely circulated. A sentence or two may be quoted :—

" I see the English constitution remaining firm ; the same Houses of Parliament ; the same taxes, customs, and excise; the same trading companies, laws, and judicatures ; whilst ours are either subjected to new regulations, or are annihilated for ever. And for what ? that we may be admitted to the honour of paying their old arrears, and presenting a few witnesses to attest the new debts, which they may be pleased to contract. Good God ! is this an entire surrender ? My heart bursts with indignation and grief, at the triumph which the English will obtain to-day, over a fierce and warlike nation that has struggled to maintain its independence so long ! "

An amendment was proposed which affirmed that the nation was averse to an incorporating union, that if it was accepted in its present form, instead of securing peace it would cause dismal distractions and confusion between the two nations and that therefore it would be best to retain the sovereignty and independence of the monarchy, the fundamental constitution of the government as established by the Claim of Right, and the laws of the kingdom. After the amendment was debated, the motion put to the House was—" Approve of the first article of the Union, yes or no." Before the vote was taken, the Duke of Athole protested for himself and his adherents, that an incorporating union as proposed in this treaty, "is contrary to the honour, the interest, the fundamental laws, and the constitution of this kingdom ; the birthright of the peers, the rights of the barons, and the boroughs, and the property and the liberty of the subjects." The first article was carried by a majority of thirty-one.

From this date to the end of December, at almost every sitting addresses and petitions were presented and read against the Union. But the treaty was pressed forward, and on the last day of November they had reached the eighth article, and remitted it with some of the preceding ones to a committee. Amendments and additions were made to some of the articles. And an act was inserted in it definitely stating that the Presbyterian Church should continue unalterable in her worship, doctrine, and government, "to the people of this land in all succeeding generations."

The parts of the treaty relating to commerce were generally satisfactory to the Scots, and adopted with slight modifications. The nineteenth article of the Union sanctioned the retention of the judicial organisation of Scotland. The weakest article of the treaty was the twentieth, which reserved all the heritable offices and the hereditary jurisdictions "to the owners thereof as rights of property."

The Jacobites determined to make their last grand effort to defeat the Union on the twenty-second article, which apportioned the share of representation from Scotland in the Imperial Parliament. It was read on the 7th of January, 1707, and the debate continued through four sittings. It was most vehemently discussed point by point, and six protests were entered against the first paragraph, which were followed by more menacing counter-protests as each part of the article was carried. But the Duke of Hamilton misled the Jacobites and disconcerted them ; and their rage and noisy proceedings were unavailing, for the article was carried. The remaining articles were passed on the 14th of January ; and on the 16th an Act was passed which ratified the Treaty of Union by a majority of forty-one.

The Union limited the representation of Scotland to forty-five members in the House of Commons of the United Kingdom, and to sixteen peers in the House of Lords.   Of the forty-five Scotch members thirty were given to the counties, and fifteen to the boroughs.   Some other matters were arranged, and an Act was passed for the preservation of game.   On the 25th of March, the royal commissioner addressed a few sentences to the members, and Parliament separated and met no more.

The treaty was placed before the English Parliament, and passed through both Houses without much opposition.   On the 6th of March, 1707, it received the royal assent, and thenceforth became a part of the Constitution of the United Kingdom.

XVII.

RISINGS OF 1715 AND 1745.

A CHANGE so vast as the Union could not be effected without rousing bitter passions in the hearts of many, which nothing but time could appease. The Jacobite party strove to enflame the discontent of the people, and to frustrate the Whigs. In Scotland they were strong and commanded considerable influence ; and their plots to restore the exiled House of Stuart were incessant. At the same time many other occasions of irritation naturally arose from commercial disputes, and in connection with the new revenue system. The English introduced their own modes of collecting duties and customs, and what was more offensive, the taxes were greatly increased.

In the later years of Queen Anne's reign, the Jacobites had gained ground. She died in August, 1714. The Elector of Hanover then ascended the throne under the title of George I. Although the Jacobites were not quite prepared to take the field, they expected external aid. The Earl of Mar acted against the Jacobites in the Union proceedings ; but he was a shifty politician, and was Secretary of State

BOTHWELL CASTLE.

in Bolingbroke's Government. When in this office he was entrusted with the distribution of sums of money among the Highland clans, which gave him some influence over the chiefs. If Mar had obtained a post in the new Government under George I. as he anxiously desired, he would not have headed a rising of the Jacobites ; but on finding himself neglected, he determined to be revenged.

Rumours of a rising were heard in May, 1715. In August, Mar assembled his friends and followers at Braemar Castle, and announced to them his scheme. He was joined by the Marquis of Huntly, the Marquis of Tullibardine, the Earls Marischal, Seaforth, Southesk, Stormont, Nithsdale, and a number of the Highland chiefs. As the rising spread some of the nobles in the north of England joined it.

Mar unfurled the standard of revolt on the 6th of September, near Braemar Castle, marched by Dunkeld, and entered Perth on the 28th with 5,000 men. In November there were 14,000 men in arms for the Stuart cause. But Mar had no military skill, and remained too long inactive in Perth. Before the arrival of James VIII., the Pretender, at Peterhead on the 22nd of December, the army had melted away to a few thousands. James, who suffered from attacks of ague in his progress southward, reached Perth on the 6th of January, 1716 ; but his presence inspired no new hope. He had not the mien of a man likely to lead an army to victory and to glory. Preparations were made for his coronation at Scone on the 23rd of January ; but when that day came, the royal army under Argyle had begun their march on Perth, and James was seriously thinking of flight.

The hapless prince and the army commenced their retreat on the 30th of January, and marched by Dundee to Montrose, where on the 4th of February, James and the Earl of Mar went aboard a French vessel and sailed for France. The insurgent army was fast diminishing as it proceeded northward, and on reaching Aberdeen, it disbanded on the 7th of February. Thus ended a project begun without requisite preparation, conducted without energy or skill, and leading to nothing but suffering and ruin to a portion of the people.

Lenient counsel toward the insurgents prevailed in Scotland, and few of them were judicially punished. But the English Government took the punishment of the prisoners and those implicated in the rising into their own hands. A large number of all ranks of men were executed ; and hundreds were sent to the plantations to drag out a wretched life in slavery. The estates of upwards of forty families in Scotland were forfeited.

Shortly after the suppression of the rising, the Government adopted measures to secure the peace of the Highlands. Acts were passed for disarming the Celtic people. General Wade planned and constructed a system of military roads. But the action of the imperial Government often irritated the Scots ; and the Jacobites still longed for the return of the banished dynasty.

The clan organisation, with a few feudal elements superposed upon it, continued in the Highlands till after the rising of 1745. Even the Lowland nobles retained their hereditary jurisdictions over their vassals. So among the causes of the rising under Prince Charles, may be enumerated the local power of the Highland chiefs and the nobles over many of the people. There were also the prejudices still existing against the Union, and an undercurrent of disaffection to England, kept alive by the memories of centuries of war and oppression. Besides, a kind of half-romantic and indescribable feeling leaning toward the ancient line of kings, undoubtedly existed and still exists in the nation. Among minor causes we must count the culpable neglect of the Government, which allowed the prince and his followers to appear for a time in a career of success.

When Prince Charles Stuart landed in the Western Isles on the 23rd of June, 1745, his prospects of success were dreary. It was some time before he found one single man to give him the least spark of hope. The Highlanders whom he first met told him and insisted that a rising was utterly impossible. But the young prince was naturally full of hope and faith in his destiny, and determined to recover the throne of his ancestors. After repeated efforts he induced a number of the chiefs to promise him support ; and on the 19th of August, he raised his standard in Glenfinnan, with upwards of a thousand men around him. Next morning they commenced their march, and were soon joined by other chiefs and their followers. As the only regular army in the kingdom under General Cope was moved from Edinburgh to Inverness, Prince Charles resolved to advance on the capital. He entered Perth on the 4th of September, and there

CHARLES EDWARD IN LATER YEARS.

his army was largely reinforced. On the 11th he recommenced his march, crossed the Forth, and took possession of Edinburgh on the 17th, amid the applause of the people.

By this time Cope had returned from Inverness, and was landing his troops at Dunbar. But the insurgents anticipated his action and advanced to meet him. The Highlanders attacked the royal army at Preston on the 21st of September, completely defeated it, and Cope fled in haste to Berwick. Many prisoners and much booty fell into the hands of the victors. The Highland army re-entered Edinburgh in triumph; and for a few weeks Charles held court at Holyrood Palace and acted as king of Scotland. But his difficulties were only beginning. He had failed to take the castle of Edinburgh, and few of the Lowland people supported his cause.

Full of confidence in his destiny, Charles, with an army of about six thousand men, commenced to march on London on the 1st of November. They took Carlisle on the 18th, and levied a contribution from the citizens. Leaving a garrison in the castle, they resumed the march on the 22nd. Few recruits joined the prince's ranks in the progress southward. They reached Manchester on the 27th, where two hundred men joined the army; but there was no indication of a great movement on Charles' side in England. They advanced to Derby, which is within one hundred and twenty miles of London, when the leaders of the army received tidings which convinced them of the fatuity of continuing the march. There were three armies in the field opposed to them, two between them and

Scotland, and one posted for the defence of London. Immediate retreat was their last chance of saving themselves from destruction. But Prince Charles was extremely unwilling to turn back, and bitterly protested against such a proposal ; he had great faith in the divine right and justice of his cause, and persisted in advancing to the climax of his destiny. The retreat was ordered on the 6th of December. The rank and file of the army rent the air with cries of indignation ; they could have endured to be defeated by superior numbers, but to retreat without striking a blow was an insufferable disgrace.

When they returned, Edinburgh was in the hands of the Government, and in other parts of the kingdom troops were organised and prepared to act against them. They retreated through Dumfries, and entered Glasgow on the 24th of December, wearied and tattered. Charles exacted a large contribution of clothing and shoes from the city, rested a week, and proceeded to Stirling. On the 17th of January, 1746, they attacked and defeated the royal force under General Hawley, at Falkirk. The Duke of Cumberland was commissioned to extinguish the rising. He arrived at Edinburgh on the 30th of January ; and, with an army of fourteen thousand men, and a train of artillery, advanced northward. Charles' army was attempting to reduce Stirling Castle when tidings of Cumberland's advance came. The insurgents then commenced a retreat, and reached Crieff on the 2nd of February. There they separated into two divisions, one, under the prince, moved by Blair Athole ; the other, under Lord George

Murray, marched by Montrose and Aberdeen. It was arranged that they should meet at Inverness. Cumberland proceeded to Aberdeen and rested his army till the spring. On the 8th of April he commenced his march for Inverness along the coast in connection with a victualling fleet, which sailed parallel with his army; and on the 14th he reached Nairn.

THE OLD TOLBOOTH TOWER, ABERDEEN.

By this time the prince's army was suffering severely from constant exposure and want of food. The men were much exhausted, and at the utmost only numbered five thousand foot, and one hundred cavalry. They were mustered on Culloden Moor; but though the most experienced chiefs earnestly entreated Charles to

avoid a battle or remove to a better position, yet he
was deaf to all reason and insisted on an immediate
action.   Thus his followers were forced to form on
the Moor behind the enclosure of Culloden House.
The Duke continued his march, and came in sight of
the insurgents.   On the 16th of April, he began the
battle by a canonade which committed much havoc
in the insurgent's ranks.   After a heroic charge and a
severe but brief combat, the clansmen were defeated
by the weight of superior numbers, and many of them
were mercilessly massacred in the pursuit.   Prince
Charles escaped, and the remnants of his army dispersed.   The victors then began an indiscriminate
slaughter of all those supposed to be disaffected to the
Government, or in any way connected with the rising.
The Duke of Cumberland and General Hawley have
entailed on themselves eternal infamy by the cruelties
which they inflicted upon the defenceless and innocent
inhabitants of the Highlands.

There was great rejoicing in London over the victory at Culloden.   But many people who were not
Jacobites, were shocked by the details of the cruelties
and sufferings inflicted on the Celtic population.   Dr.
Smollett, the well-known novelist, gave expression to
this feeling in his poem, entitled " The Tears of Scotland," of which the following lines are a specimen :—

> " Mourn, hapless Caledonia, mourn,
> Thy banished peace, thy laurels torn !
> Thy sons, for valour long renowned,
> Lie slaughtered on their native ground ;
> Thy hospitable roofs no more
> Invite the stranger to the door ;

45, GUEST ROW, ABERDEEN, INHABITED BY THE DUKE OF CUMBERLAND.

In smoky ruins sunk they lie,
The monuments of cruelty.

*   *   *   *   ⁂   ⁂

Oh ! baneful cause, oh ! fatal morn,
Accursed to ages yet unborn ;
The sons against their fathers stood,
The parent shed his children's blood.
Yet, when the rage of battle ceased,
The victor's soul was not appeased :
The naked and forlorn must feel
Devouring flames and murdering steel.

The pious mother, doomed to death,
Forsaken wanders o'er the heath,
The bleak winds whistle round her head,
Her helpless orphans cry for bread ;
Bereft of shelter, food, and friend,
She views the shades of night descend ;
And stretched beneath the inclement skies
Weeps o'er her tender babes, and dies."

From the Revolution to the suppression of the last rising, the rhymes and ballads were the common outcome of the rhymers of the street, the alehouse, the club, the festival board, the farmhouse, and the cot, amongst the valleys and the hills. The Jacobites always endeavoured to catch the ear of the people, and constantly appealed to the lighter emotions, the passions, and the selfish feelings under the guise of a mass of rough humour and coarse satire—thrown at the new dynasty and the Whigs—the alleged authors of all the woes of the nation. After the battle of Culloden a higher strain was struck. The bitterness of defeat, of suffering, and of sorrow, filled the souls of the Jacobites and inspired them with a mournful and yet noble resolution to yield to their fate, and make the best of the changed circumstances. There are a large number of these later Jacobite songs and ballads. Some of them are beautiful and exceedingly touching, and still popular in Scotland.

XVIII

GENERAL RESULT OF THE OPERATION OF THE UNION.

LOOKING at the Union as means to an end, we find it had a vast effect on the welfare of the people. At once it greatly widened the field of commercial enterprise to the Scots, and directly tended to afford them more security in every quarter of the globe. The Scots always had a fund of energy and ample power of endurance, but external obstacles had long retarded their progress and crippled their best efforts. Hence, when the nation was placed under more favourable conditions by the Union, the people advanced rapidly in wealth and civilisation.

It was the earnest desire of the Scots to obtain equal commercial rights which made the Union possible and endurable. Though (as we shall see) the first attempts to adjust the fiscal relations of the two kingdoms caused disturbance, still it was ultimately beneficial. Another most important arrangement was the coinage. In 1708 the Scottish coins were finally called in, and preparations were made for a coinage exactly on the method of the

English mint. Thus one of the good results of the Union was soon obtained ; as the convenience and advantage of only one coinage and standard of money for the island is obvious.

Prior to the Union the Scots were permitted to trade only where the English Government thought fit. But after it there was no limitation, their ships might trade with the remotest quarters of the world. The splendid ships and fine steamers which have steered from the ports of Scotland for

MONUMENT TO C. H. BELL (THE BUILDER OF THE FIRST STEAM VESSEL) ON THE BANKS OF THE CLYDE.

several generations afford ample evidence of the energy, the skill, and the enterprise of her sons. Since the Union the development of shipping and shipbuilding, has been vast and varied. Shipbuilding itself has passed through several revolutions in which Scotland has taken a leading part. It may, therefore, be affirmed that the Union commercially has been highly beneficial, and that the advantages flowing from it have tended to promote the prosperity and

THE CLYDE MAKER AT WORK.

the material development of the natural resources of the country.

Although the Scots relinquished their separate legislative power, they gained a position and a share in the government of a larger nation, and in the honour and glory of the British Empire. As they retained their own laws and legal organisations, and their religious and educational institutions, the great change implied in the Union embraced many elements of moral advantage. Scotch nationality and patriotism have continued essentially unimpaired, but much of its prejudice and narrowness which the strife of preceding ages had generated, has been slowly thrown off. It is always true that a people's own country and affairs are of prime importance to them ; yet a people that limited all their faculties and energies to the internal affairs of their own country, would be emphatically characterised as a narrow-minded, a poor, and an unsympathetic community. If all our political institutions and social organisations were expressly framed and exclusively directed to this one end, it would manifest a weak and a contemptible ideal of humanity. From these and many other considerations, it appears to me that the Union afforded great and inestimable moral advantages to Scotland. And the records of the last hundred years show that Scotsmen have fully appreciated and enjoyed these advantages.

The Union conferred many advantages, and also entailed disadvantages, in political and legislative relations. It might be assumed that the united deliberation and counsel of the British Parliament would be more competent to frame wise and useful legislation than a Scotch Parliament. This would depend on the accuracy of the information which the British Parliament possessed of the opinions and convictions of the Scotch people and of their institutions, and, from a lack of this, has occasionally inflicted pain and injustice on the people of Scotland. An instructive instance occurred after the first rising, touching the disposal of the forfeited estates. Parliament placed the control of the matter in the hands of a Commission, which proceeded to sell the estates. A number of creditors who had claims on the estates applied to the Court of Session, and sequestration was granted. The commissioners failed to understand this proceeding, and complained to the Government that they were prevented from discharging their duty by a body calling itself the Court of Session ; they therefore asked the Government to increase their powers. And the British Parliament passed an Act which ignored the jurisdiction of the Court of Session, in direct violation of the stipulations of the Union, and in spite of the protest of the Scotch judges.

In finance and fiscal arrangements the British Parliament has not generally treated Scotland worse than England. For a generation or two after the Union much irritation was caused by changes and rearrangements in this branch of government, and a few examples may be narrated. Ale was a staple necessary in the domestic economy and trade of the nation. At the time of the Union there was no malt tax in Scotland, but there was a duty on liquor. In

1713 a malt tax of 6d. per bushel was imposed upon Scotland, though the Scotch members in both Houses of Parliament bitterly opposed it. At this date there were upwards of five thousand maltsters in Scotland ; and in June the tax was ordered to be enforced. " But such was the general and determined resolution of the inhabitants not to submit, that the officers of excise for several years were everywhere refused access to survey and charge the duty ; and that when charged it was never paid, nor could it be recovered by proceedings at law, as the justices of peace in all the counties refused to act. The consequence was that, during the twelve years after the 24th of June, 1713, while the tax continued at 6d. per bushel, the duty actually levied amounted to a mere trifle, and fell considerably short of the necessary expense attending this branch of the revenue."

In 1724 the Government wished to raise £20,000 by a tax on Scotch ale. Parliament passed an Act proposing to levy 6d. per barrel on ale instead of the malt tax, and to exclude the Scots from the bounty on exported grain, which was to be continued in England. The nation vehemently resented the proposal, and protested against it. It was relinquished, and a malt tax of 3d. per bushel imposed. As £20,000 had to be drawn from the Scots, it was enacted that, if the tax of 3d. failed to produce the amount, it must be made up by a surcharge on maltsters.

The Act came into operation in June, 1725, and the citizens of Glasgow manifested a sullen attitude when the excisemen were preparing to enforce it. The following day they appeared in crowds on the streets ; the magistrates failed to disperse them, and a party of soldiers were called into the city. Shouts were raised against Campbell of Shawfield, their member of parliament, who was suspected of having assisted the Government. They said, as he had already betrayed them, now he was to enslave them beneath a military yoke, and slay them if they resisted. At night they attacked his house and laid it in ruins. Next morning the mob appeared and jeered at the soldiers on guard. Their commander ordered them to turn out and form square, and, without the authority of the provost, commanded them to fire on the crowd. Eight of the citizens were killed and many wounded. The crisis was reached. The people ran to an old armoury, and having armed themselves, at once presented so threatening a front that it was feared all the soldiers would be massacred, and the officer marched them to Dumbarton. A regiment of infantry, seven troops of dragoons, and a company of Highlanders from General Wade's force, were sent into Glasgow, and quietness was restored. Criminal proceedings were instituted, the magistrates of Glasgow were seized and imprisoned in Edinburgh. The charges against them were abandoned, but a few of the rioters were punished The captain in command of the party who fired upon the crowd, was tried and condemned, but received a royal pardon. The citizens of Glasgow were deeply offended, and the Jacobites were exceedingly jubilant.

In Edinburgh the opposition to the malt tax assumed a determined form. All the brewers resolved to cease brewing. The Lord Advocate lodged a complaint against them in the Court of Session, and the Court ordered them to proceed with their work as usual. They refused, and some of them were imprisoned ; but at last they yielded. These proceedings were only the first of a series of excise difficulties which continued for more than a hundred years. In some parts of the north and west of the kingdom smuggling whisky was common till past the first quarter of the present century. The smuggling brewing houses were often beside a fresh spring or stream of water, in out-of-the-way glens and hill-sides, where no one could see them without searching carefully ; in general, they were small and rudely constructed. The whisky smuggler usually stored his malt in a square pit on a hill among long heather and at some distance from his brewing house.

The malt tax continued at from 3d. to 7d. per bushel till the end of last century. In 1802 it was raised to 1s. 8d. per bushel, which caused universal complaints in Scotland. The following year the tax was raised to 3s. 8d. per bushel, which occasioned a great outcry throughout the kingdom, though the tax was 8d. per bushel more in England than in Scotland. But the effect of this enormous increase of the tax on the cultivation of Scotch bere or barley was immediately ruinous. And in 1804 Sir John Sinclair stated: "The malt duties lately imposed seem to have been intended to annihilate the cultivation of this grain altogether ; it would be but spending time to no purpose to express anything on the subject. We may indeed

continue to grow a little of it for the purpose of
feeding our horses, or feeding our poor people, but
as to making it into malt, that appears to be
altogether out of the question, as the demand for it
for that purpose has not merely declined, but ceased
altogether ; insomuch that, had it not been for a few
cargoes of it that were taken off our hands this season
to feed the people that were starving in Shetland and
in Norway, we might have dunged our land with it for
any other market that this country now affords." It
was further recorded that the use of ale and beer had
been very generally relinquished over whole districts ;
and that the extinguishing of the Scotch farmer's
market for his principal crop was reducing his
ability to cultivate the land, and rendering him less
able to pay his rents and taxes, and less capable
of serving, as well as less serviceable to the community by producing the necessaries of life.

Of Scotch whisky, which has long been famous
50,844 gallons were produced in 1708.   In 1756 there
were 433,811 gallons; but then the duty was increased,
which caused a fall in the production.   Shortly after
a demand for Scotch whisky arose in England, and
large quantities of it were transmitted there ; but an
import duty of 2s. 6d. a gallon was imposed, which
was quickly followed by a system of smuggling.
It is said that in 1787, upwards of 300,000 gallons
of Scotch whisky crossed the Border without
the cognisance of the excise.   A new mode of
charging the duty on spirits was tried in 1786, the
licence duty being calculated upon the capacity of
the stills.   But the distillers soon altered the form

of the stills, and increased the rate of production. When the Government discovered this, the amount of the licence was raised year by year, till in 1798 it amounted to £64 16s. 4d. per gallon of still capacity. The mode of charging the duty was again changed in 1799, when a duty of 4s. 10¼d. was put on each gallon of spirits produced for home consumption. There were then eighty-seven licensed distillers in Scotland, but they diapproved of the change, and many of them gave up business, so the amount of duty fell off for a year or two. In 1802 the Government reduced the duty to 3s. 10½d. per gallon. In 1803 there were eighty-eight distillers, who paid a duty of £2,022,409. The next year the duty was raised, and the number of distillers decreased, till in 1813 there were only twenty-four ; at this time the duty was 9s. 4½d. per gallon. In 1823 it was lowered to 2s. 4¾d. per gallon, when the number of distillers greatly increased, and the revenue accordingly rose. In 1833 the rate of duty was 3s. 4½d. a gallon, and the number of distillers 243, who paid a duty of £5,988,556. In 1840 the duty was 3s. 8d., the number of distillers 205, and the quantity of whisky produced 9,032,353 gallons. The same year the quantity of spirits charged with duty as consumed in Scotland was 6,007,631 gallons. In 1855 the quantity of whisky produced was 11,283,636 gallons. In 1867 there were 111 distillers, and the whisky produced was 10,813,996 gallons, and the same year the quantity of spirits charged with duty as consumed in Scotland was 4,983,000 gallons.

In 1748 the Imperial Parliament abolished hereditary jurisdictions in Scotland, which were associated with the ownership of land and titles of rank. It was a wise measure, but it should have been passed immediately after Mar's rising. The forfeited estates of the nobles and chiefs implicated in the rising of 1745 were pretty well managed by a board of commissioners ; and a part of the proceeds drawn from them were applied to public improvements. The Highland Society, instituted in 1784, received a grant of £3,000, and £50,000 was lent to complete the Forth and Clyde Canal, which the proprietors of the canal repaid before 1806. £25,000 was lent for completing the Crinan Canal ; and a like sum to the magistrates of Edinburgh to improve the harbour of Leith ; and £1,000 to erect a prison in Inverness. In 1784 the estates were restored to the heirs of the former owners, under the condition that they should repay the sums paid by the public on account of the debts due by the persons whose estates had been forfeited, which amounted to upwards of £90,000.

In the closing years of the last and the opening years of the present century there was a spirit of emigration in the Highlands. The Highland Society, in the years 1801, 1802, and 1803, transmitted several reports giving detailed information to the Government, touching the means of diverting the rage for emigration which prevailed ; they strongly urged the Government to encourage public works, such as the Caledonian Canal, and the construction of roads and bridges in the Highlands. In 1803 Parliament passed an Act authorising a sum of £20,000 for making roads and bridges in the Highlands, and enabling landowners to encumber their estates with a portion of the expense of such works. The Government had employed Mr. Telford, the eminent engineer, to survey and report on the state of the roads and bridges, and on the means of promoting the fisheries on the east and west coasts, with the object of preventing further emigration of the inhabitants of the Highlands. He collected a vast mass of interesting and important facts, and presented his report in April, 1803 ; and in summer he received instructions to prepare for practical operations. He proceeded to the Highlands, planned the lines of roads and bridges which were most necessary, and aimed at securing the connection of the new lines of roads by bridges at the most important points, such as Dunkeld, over the Tay. The bridge of Dunkeld, which forms the opening to the central Highlands, was finished in 1809, and the communication to the north of Inverness was continued by a bridge over the Beauly. He also erected important bridges to connect the existing lines of roads—one at Ballater over the Dee, another at Alford over the Don, and one at Craigellachie over the Spey. Having thus connected the main lines of roads, he concentrated his attention upon the interior of the Highlands. And by the year 1820, twelve hundred new bridges were erected, and nine hundred and twenty miles of good roads were added to the means of communication in this region. The first stage coaches which ran northward from Perth to Inverness were tried in 1808 ; before 1811 they were

SCUIR NA-GILLIAN.

regularly established; and in 1820 forty stage coaches arrived in Inverness every week, and as many departed.

The Caledonian Canal, also the work of Telford, was opened in 1822.   It is needless to say that since that time there has been a complete revolution in the means of communication both on sea and land : nevertheless, the opening up of the Highlands was an important step in the Story of Scotland.

In the last century there was no popular representation in Scotland.   The town councils elected the borough members of parliament ; and in 1790, the total number of voters in all the counties of the kingdom was only 2,652.   In those days it was an easy matter for the Government to manage the elections as they thought fit, and they did so.   The press was only in its infancy : a hard and bitter contest had to be fought ere it obtained freedom of discussion. Corporations and public bodies might speak for themselves ; but the opinion of the general community was not recognised as having any claim to be heard or consulted.   The Government recognised no public opinion save that which issued from themselves or their official organs.   So long as the people plodded on quietly at their daily occupations, the corruption of the political fabric was concealed behind its official trappings.   But, when the French Revolution burst out, it sent a shock of alarm and panic into the heart of every government in Europe.

Its effects soon appeared in the administration of Scotland.   The terror of revolution seized the British Government ; reason itself shook, and justice and humanity were driven beyond the gates of mercy. Everything rung with the French Revolution, which was made the all-in-all for about twenty years. "Everything, not this or that, but literally everything, was soaked in this one event." Although there is no evidence that any considerable number of persons in Scotland ever embraced the French revolutionary principles, there were many people who desired to reform the existing political system of government. But the reigning Toryism, in order to retain its monopoly of power, fixed upon all reformers and opponents the stigma of Jacobins, revolutionaries, and seditious persons. There were but few real Whigs in Scotland, and they were viewed by the Government with extreme suspicion : even Dugald Stewart, the fluent professor of moral philosophy in Edinburgh, was an object of great secret alarm. All persons who held liberal opinions were subjected to contumely, insult, and personal loss and danger for many years.

The Government suppressed all attempts to form political associations. It employed a set of spies who often brought innocent and unsuspecting persons into the iron grasp of the criminal law. When any government expressly pays men to discover sedition among a peaceful community, these men in the interest of their trade will soon create a show of the article required by their employers : this was what happened in Scotland. A number of men were seized, imprisoned, and accused of sedition, tried, convicted, and sentenced to death or transportation. At one of these political trials the Lord Justice

Clerk in his address to the jury laid it down as an unquestionable doctrine—" That the British Constitution is the best that ever was since the creation of the world, and it is impossible to make it better." After that there was nothing more to be said, since all reform was futile.

Liberal principles and freedom of discussion slowly advanced in Scotland. First the better classes of tradesmen, next the middle and commercial class, and then the Whigs raised their voice in parliament. Signs began to appear which convinced those in authority that their lease of power was not eternal. Still the body of the people were for long left outside of the constitution ; they had to fight more than a generation ere they obtained political rights.

If we look to the change of conditions and circumstances arising from the extension and the development of the British Empire since the Union, the greater complexity of internal organisation, and the advance of civilisation in the United Kingdom, it may easily be seen that the Imperial Government of 1707 had a much narrower range of business, and less difficult problems to deal with, than fall to the lot of the Government of the present day. In the present century there have been revolutions in governments, in commerce, in the means of warfare, in industry, in the means of communication, and also in thought and belief. It is idle to imagine that the legislative apparatus and constitution of the past, is competent to master and to treat the political and social problems of the present.

XIX.

THE ideas of the Scotch Reformers were not elaborated at once ; religion and secular government were often mixed in the early stages of the Reformation movement. A Church distinct from and independent of the State was an idea quite alien to the forms of thought which prevailed amongst the Reformers ; on the other hand, a secular government distinct from and independent of the Church was a conception scarcely entertained by any statesman of the sixteenth or seventeenth centuries. The common notions of theocracy were held by the Church and State as being both under the direction of God, and therefore requiring to be associated. The theocratic idea is grand and inspiring in contemplation. But in practical operation it appears that the Church and the State both claim a supremacy : and they often hold very different views as to what is the will of God, or how far and in what circumstances the word of God should be followed. The king may maintain that he alone under God has a supremacy over the Church, and everything else within his dominions, as was done by James VI., Charles I., Charles II., and James VII. Whoever wishes to understand the many struggles of the Church of Scotland should form a clear conception of the theocratic principle.

According to the historic polity of the Church, the doctrine of the spiritual and civil powers were as follows :—" This power and ecclesiastical polity is different and distinct from that which is called the civil power, and belongs to the civil government of the commonwealth ; although they are both of God and tend to the same end, if they be rightly used, namely, to advance the glory of God, and to have good subjects. This ecclesiastical power flows immediately from God and the Mediator, Christ Jesus, and is spiritual, not having a temporal head on earth, but only Christ, the spiritual King and Governor of His Church. Therefore this power and polity of the Church should lean upon the Word of God immediately, as the only ground thereof, and should be taken from the pure fountains of the Scriptures, hearing the voice of Christ, the only spiritual King, and being ruled by His laws. . . . The civil power should command the spiritual to exercise and perform their office according to the Word of God. The spiritual rulers should require the Christian magistrates to administer justice and punish vice ; and to maintain the liberty and peace of the Church within their bound. . . . The magistrate ought to assist, maintain, and fortify the jurisdiction of the Church. The ministers ought to assist their princes in all things agreeable to the Word of God, provided they do not neglect their own charge by involving themselves in civil affairs."

This theory is grounded on the assumption that the Church and the State ought to assist each other, and runs on the lines of a co-ordinate jurisdiction. As to supremacy in the case of the Church, the final appeal is to the word of God, and Christ, the Head and King ; in other words, it is a distinct development of the theocratic conception. The ideas involved in the theory are irreconcilable in practical operation, unless under peculiar conditions and circumstances of society.

Touching the election of ministers to congregations, it is expressly stated, that care should always be taken not to intrude any minister on a congregation if they are not satisfied with him. Hence lay patronage was throughout inconsistent with the conception and the fundamental principles of the Presbyterian Church, and she opposed and rejected it, and fought against it. It was abolished shortly after the Revolution of 1688, but again restored by the British Parliament in 1712, contrary to the letter and the spirit of the Treaty of Union, and to all conceptions of a wise policy toward the Scottish nation.

After this the struggles of the Church were mainly internal, although they still sprang from the theory of her powers. The sentiments and feelings engendered by many years of persecution continued to be represented in the Church courts ; and hence an internal struggle arose between the party who held firmly to these sentiments and the new party —called " the Moderate party." At first the difference between the two was slight ; but in the middle of the eighteenth century the opposite views of the popular and the moderate parties had become distinct.

The chief point of polity in dispute was the settlement of ministers in parishes against the wishes of the congregations. Cases of this character were constantly coming before the presbyteries and general assemblies ; and in 1733, it was on matters arising from such cases that a secession took place. Ebenezer Erskine, minister of Stirling, was a vehement and able advocate of popular election, and in a sermon at the opening of the Synod in 1732, he stated that : " There is a twofold call necessary for a man's meddling as a builder in the Church of God—there is the call of God and of His Church. God's call consists in qualifying a man for his work. . . . The call of the Church lies in the free choice and election of the Christian people. The promise of conduct and counsel in the choice of men that are to build is not made to patrons or to any set of men, but to the Church, the body of Christ, to whom apostles, prophets, pastors, and teachers are given. As it is the natural privilege of every house or society of men to have the choice of their own servants, so it is the privilege of the house of God in particular. What a miserable bondage would it be reckoned for any family to have servants imposed on them by strangers, who might give the children a stone for bread, or a scorpion instead of a fish, or poison instead of medicine ! And shall we suppose that ever God granted a power to any set of men—patrons or whatever they be, to impose servants on His family ? "

Erskine was sharply rebuked by the synod and the General Assembly for the sentiments uttered in his sermon. But he adhered to every word of it, and protested at every stage of the proceedings against him, with three of his brethren who joined him. They boldly repelled every attempt of the assembly to threaten or to coerce them. At last, in 1740, they were turned out of their churches and manses but several years before this they had formed a pres- bytery. Dissent continued to increase, and in 1773, there were upwards of two hundred dissenting congregations, besides Episcopalians and Roman Catholics.

The question of patronage and the intrusion of presentees on reclaiming congregations occupied much of the time of the Church courts. In 1752 Dr. Robertson, the historian, inaugurated a movement for the enforcement of the law of patron- age. His policy had a most deadening tendency, inasmuch as those who adopted it had no higher principle than that of a cringing allegiance to the patrons. So this party soon lost the confidence and the respect of the people, because they had cast off the historic glory of their Church. Dr. Robertson retired from the management of Church affairs in 1780.

In 1781 the synod of Glasgow and Ayr presented overtures to the General Assembly touching patron- age, which insisted that no call should be sustained unless it was signed by a majority of the heritors, elders, and communicants of the parish. The assembly dismissed the proposal, because it was of a dangerous tendency. The synods of Dumfries, Perth and Stirling overtured the assembly to state exactly what was meant by a call; but this was simply dismissed without comment. In 1783 the synods of Perth and Stirling, and Fife, implored the assembly to make the utmost effort to get patronage repealed. The moderate party tried hard to avoid a debate; but the popular party proposed that presbyteries should be instructed to consult with the landed gentry, and report to the next assembly. In the debate it was emphatically stated that the aversion of the people to patronage was invincible, and could never be overcome.

A great revolution was preparing. The changed conditions and circumstances of society had rendered the theocratic conception impracticable, while the fundamental principles of Presbyterianism were almost incomprehensible to politicians and lawyers beyond the Tweed. Hence their futile and laughable efforts to check the evolution of the movement.

As an attempt to redress the evils involved in patronage, the popular party proposed, in the assembly of 1833, that when a majority of a con-gregation objected to the minister presented by the patron, the presbytery should not proceed with the settlement. The proposal was debated at great length; both parties exerted themselves to the utmost. Dr. Cook moved that the proposal should be adopted, and it was carried. The assembly of 1834 passed it into an act; and its effect was that when a clear majority of the male heads of families, being members of the congregation and in communion with the Church, deliberately objected to the presentee's settlement as their minister, in that case the presbytery of the district should not proceed to thrust him upon the congregation. This rule is elsewhere called " The Veto Act." It was on this reasonable regulation that the struggle which issued in the Disruption was fought, although there were other principles involved in the contest.

Without entering into many details I shall present the leading steps of the movement. In 1834 the Earl of Kinnoull presented Mr. Robert Young to the parish church of Auchterarder, in Perthshire, and the presbytery of the district, proceeding in the usual form to admit him, found that only two of the congregation had signed his call, and therefore decided that they could not induct him. The case was brought before the Court of Session, and the judges decided that the presbytery had acted contrary to the statute of 1712. This decision was appealed to the House of Lords, which asserted that the jurisdiction of the civil court is supreme, and affirmed the judgment of the Court of Session. This settled the point that the rejection of a patron's presentee on the ground of the dissent of the congregation was illegal. It also implied the conclusion that the congregation had no legal standing in the settlement of their ministers ; their only duty was to submit quietly to whoever the patron thought fit to place over them.

The General Assembly met on May 16, 1839, and intimation of the grounds of the final contest was given. Dr. Cook, the leader of the moderate party, announced that his followers had resolved to conduct the affairs of the Church in accordance with the decrees of the civil courts. Dr. Chalmers said that he would submit a motion to the assembly. The debates were long and exceedingly animated. Dr. Cook insisted that " The Veto Act," by the decision of the courts, was rendered null, as the Church had been acting under an error as to her power. Dr. Chalmers's motion was that the Church bowed to the decision of the court, so far as matters of civil right were concerned, but he avowed that : " Whereas the principle of non-intrusion is one coeval with the Reformed Church of Scotland, and forms an integral part of its constitution, embodied in its standards, and declared in various acts of assembly, the General Assembly resolved that this principle cannot be abandoned, and that no presentee should be forced upon any parish contrary to the will of the congregation." This motion was carried by a majority of forty-nine, and a deputation from the committee appointed under it proceeded to London to consult with the Government. The Government were unwilling to attempt to legislate on the points in dispute, and their almost utter ignorance of the subject was a reason for their apathy. So little were the Government aware of the facts of the case that they never dreamed of such an event as the Disruption.

It was evident that the crisis was nearing its issue, when, in 1839, the seven rebellious ministers of Strathbogie were suspended to prevent them from proceeding with the settlement of Mr. Edwards, in

DR. CHALMERS.

the parish of Marnoch. The suspended ministers placed their faith in the Court of Session, and exhibited great energy. They first obtained an interdict to prevent the minority of the presbytery, and others, from using any of the churches, churchyards, or schoolhouses, in executing the sentence which the assembly had pronounced against them. They next obtained a warrant from the court authorising them to continue to exercise all the functions of the ministry.

The General Assembly met in May, 1840, and the popular party assumed a firm attitude. The suspension of the Strathbogie ministers was sustained by a majority of eighty-four, but the debate was extremely vehement. The moderate party maintained that the Church must submit to the dictation of the civil courts, as this was the law of the land, and obedience to it the first duty of all loyal subjects.

Under an order from the Court of Session the suspended ministers of Strathbogie inducted Mr. Edwards in the church of Marnoch, on January 21, 1841. The majority of the General Assembly were driven into a position which rendered any compromise impossible ; so they deposed the Strathbogie ministers. For several years the country rang with the clamour and talk of non-intrusion and spiritual independence, and the excitement was intense. Pamphlets, speeches, and ballads were circulated through the kingdom in hundreds of thousands. The engrossing subject attracted the attention of every household, and many a family became divided in religious sentiments.   As the agitation, the controversy, and hot discussion approached its climax, the non-intrusion party repeatedly sounded the kingdom by platform speeches and open-air meetings.

When the General Assembly of 1842 met the anarchy of the Church was painful.   Under a warrant from the Court of Session the deposed ministers of Strathbogie elected two of their number, and an elder from Aberdeen, to represent them in the assembly ; but on a division their members were rejected by a majority of one hundred and thirty.   The deposed ministers went further, and interdicted the members elected by the other party in the presbytery ; but the assembly ignored this, and the members took their seats.   A motion to abolish patronage was proposed and carried by a majority of sixty-nine.   The Claim of Right was moved and debated at great length, and finally carried by a majority of one hundred and thirty-one.   The Claim is an able and well-known document.   It was drawn up by Mr. Alexander Dunlop, advocate, a wise and resolute gentleman ; he gave much of his time and thought to the service of the Church, for which he never accepted a single farthing. He was one of the ablest and calmest men who appeared in the assemblies of the period.

But the attitude and the claims of the Church of Scotland were misunderstood and misrepresented in Parliament. On 7th and 8th of March, 1843, a debate in the House of Commons took place on the Church of Scotland's Claim of Right. The subject was introduced by Mr. Fox Maule, in a very clear and able speech.   Sir James Graham followed with a rambling harangue, in which he asserted in the most dogmatic style that the Claims of the Church of Scotland were opposed to law, to order, and to common sense, " and therefore the sooner that the House extinguished them the better." Others spoke in favour and against the claims of the Church. But the Prime Minister, Sir Robert Peel, was vehemently opposed to her claims, although it is very evident that he had not taken the trouble to understand them. He solemnly declared that the Church, in its proceedings against the Strathbogie ministers, had laid claim to greater powers than ever were advanced, even before the Reformation, by the Church of Rome. Touching the question of the limits of the civil and ecclesiastical powers, he thought that this should be determined by the English law lords. On a division the motion was rejected by a majority of one hundred and thirty-five ; and out of the thirty-seven Scotch members who were present, twenty-five voted in favour of the motion. Thus the British Parliament rejected the Claim of Rights, though it was approved by the representatives of Scotland.

On April 5th Lord Campbell introduced five resolutions in the House of Lords of the following character :—1. That the House of Lords was desirous that the Church of Scotland should freely enjoy her rights, government, discipline, and privileges, according to law, in all time coming. 2. That she is an excellent Church. 3. That, with a view to heal the unhappy dissensions prevailing, this House is of opinion that the demands of the Church should be conceded by the Legislature, in so far as they can be safely conceded ; and that when any measure for correcting the alleged abuses of patronage shall be constitutionally brought before this House, this House will favourably entertain the same, and anxiously endeavour that the end of the said measure may be attained. 4. That in the opinion of this House the demand that patronage should be abolished as a grievance is unreasonable and unfounded, and ought not to be conceded. 5. That the demand of the Church that the law should be so framed as to give her courts absolute authority in every case, to define the limits of their own jurisdiction, without any power in any civil court in any way to question or interfere with her proceedings or decrees, although they may exceed their jurisdiction, is unprecedented in any Christian Church since the Reformation, is inconsistent with the permanent welfare of the Church, and the existence of subordinate and good government of the country.

In the debate the speakers maintained that no redress should be given until the Church obeyed the existing law. Lord Brougham said, " he would not be a party to the suicidal, to the self-destructive folly, of giving men new laws to break until they consented to obey the old law." Referring to Lord Aberdeen, he said, "his noble friend who seemed to be a non-intrusionist. What? Would he have that principle not only established in Scotland, but carried south of the Tweed ? Would he have it eat into our English system ? Would he seek, by means of it, to destroy our Erastianism ? " Such was the twaddle vented in the House of Lords ; not a glimpse of what was due to the people of Scotland entered their minds.

The popular party were everywhere preparing to leave the Establishment, as it was now hopeless to prolong the contest. The forethought, the systematic order, the discipline of the rank and file of the clergy, and the completeness of all their arrangements, were really wonderful. The final scene of leaving the Establishment presented the characteristics of the closing act of a noble and well-played drama.

On the two Sundays before the meeting of the assembly, many congregations throughout the country were deeply affected by farewell sermons from the ministers to whom they were warmly attached. It was well known that a startling move was to be made, but the uncertainty of its form and extent caused an anxiety and uneasiness of feeling unexampled since the Union. How would the royal commissioner act? Would he dissolve the assembly? Or would he recognise the minority as constituting it?

The assembly met on the 18th of May, 1843. Dr. Welsh of Edinburgh opened the proceedings, and delivered a sermon in St. Giles, in which he announced what was going to happen. He then proceeded to St. Andrew's Church, where the assembly was to be held, and took his place in the Moderator's chair; and a few minutes later the royal commissioner entered. The church was crowded, and Dr. Welsh rose and engaged in prayer. After the members had resumed their seats, he again rose, and announced :—
" That in consequence of certain proceedings affecting their rights and privileges, which had been sanctioned by the Government of the country ; and more espe-

EDINBURGH.

cially seeing that there had been an infringement on the liberties of the constitution of the Church, so that they could not constitute this court without violating the terms of the union between the Church and the State in this nation, therefore I protest against our proceeding further." Amidst profound silence and intense alarm on the opposition benches, he read the protest, which fully explained the grounds of the step they were about to take. When he had finished reading it, he handed it to the clerk at the table, bowed to the royal commissioner, quitted the chair, lifted his hat, and walked away. Instantly Dr. Chalmers, Dr. Gordon, and the whole of those in the left side of the church, rose and followed him. Upwards of two hundred ministers walked out, and they were joined outside by three hundred clergymen and other adherents.

Dr. Welsh wore his Moderator's dress, and when he appeared on the street, and the people saw that principle had risen above interest, shouts of triumph rent the air such has had not been heard in Edinburgh since the days of the Covenant. They walked through Hanover Street to Canonmills, where a large hall was erected for the reception of the disestablished assembly. They elected Dr. Chalmers moderator, and formed the first General Assembly of "The Free Church of Scotland." Four hundred and seventy-four ministers left the Establishment in 1843 ; they were also joined by two hundred probationers, nearly one hundred theological students of the University of Edinburgh, three-fourths of those in Glasgow, and a majority of those in Aberdeen.

The Disruption was an accomplished fact. I call it

21

a revolution of a high character, as it was effected without violence or bloodshed. It was an event charged with a moral power of vast import, which could not fail to produce beneficial results. The Free Church commenced her work with vigour and earnestness, and her success from the first has been remarkable.

The Established Church for a time was greatly crippled, and her pre-eminence has not been restored, although she has worked steadily and well, and extended her lines considerably. The Roman Catholics in recent years have relatively increased more than any other denomination ; and the hierarchy was restored in Scotland in 1878. Toleration and freedom of thought have made almost incredible progress in Scotland within the last fifty years ; and no one need now be afraid to announce his opinions and sentiments if he has anything to tell worth attention

XX.

MODERN LITERATURE OF SCOTLAND.

THE political and religious contests of the seventeenth century were extremely unfavourable to literary culture. In the succeeding century circumstances became more propitious, and greater literary activity was displayed. Style was made a special object of study. The critical examination of historical evidence began to be recognised, and the real requisites of historical inquiry better appreciated and understood.

David Hume was filled with a passionate love of literary fame, and turned aside from his philosophical speculations to try his skill in historic composition. His "History of Great Britain," which extended to six volumes, was at first bitterly assailed by the Whigs of the day ; but it soon became popular, new editions appeared in rapid succession, and he was placed in the front rank of English historians. Although he was highly gifted and well qualified to estimate every kind of historical evidence, he allowed himself to fall into some mistakes and inconsistencies. He was constitutionally disqualified from forming fair and just opinions on the Covenanting struggle and the period of the persecution, or from realising the position of his suffering countrymen. While he shows a lamentable deficiency in appreciating many of the genuine influences of the seventeenth century, yet on other occasions the views of conflicting parties are

HUME'S GRAVE.

grasped and presented with rare power and fairness. His form of narration is admirable. He fully recognised the importance of culture, and devoted certain portions of his history to it. His style is exceedingly clear, easy, graceful, and polished.

Dr. William Robertson, a minister of the Church of Scotland, attained a wide reputation as a historian. His chief works are the " History of Scotland," and " History of the Reign of Charles V. of Spain." He shows considerable realistic power and good judgment. The historic works of Hume and Robertson formed an era in Scotch literature ; they cleared the ground and swept in front of all their British predecessors : insomuch, that Gibbon who followed, only wished to rank with them—" The perfect composition, the nervous language, and the well-turned periods of Dr. Robertson, inflamed me to the ambitious hope that I might one day tread in his footsteps."

Patrick F. Tytler was the author of a " History of Scotland," and many other works, chiefly of a biographical character. His " History of Scotland " evinces much original research and great industry. His style is plain and animated, but somewhat diffuse.

Sir Archibald Alison's " History of Europe," which covers the period from the commencement of the French Revolution to the accession of Napoleon in 1852, has some historic merit, and has been translated into most of the European languages. His mastery of arrangement was creditable, his narration fresh and animated, and his description realistic and interesting.

Dr. John H. Burton produced a large number of works, chiefly on legal, biographical, and historical subjects ; most of which were valuable and interesting contributions to the literature of Scotland. His longest work is the " History of Scotland," from

Agricola's invasion to the suppression of the rising in
1745. One of his latest efforts was a "History of
the Reign of Queen Anne." He was an able, an
instructive, and an indefatigable writer.

The works of Thomas Carlyle extend over various
fields of literature, translations from the German,
critical essays, political and satirical pamphlets, biography, and history. He is the author of many

THOMAS CARLYLE.

volumes, and commands the attention and admiration
of a large body of readers. His chief works in the
historic branch which he cultivated were, "The
French Revolution ; " " Oliver Cromwell's Letters and
Speeches;" and the "History of Frederick II., called
the Great." "The French Revolution" is the best
of his historic works. His powers of description

were amazing, and he presents a realistic and seething panorama of the Revolution. " Frederick II." is the longest of his works, and extends to six large volumes. There is much patient research in it, vivid touches on men and things, sage remarks, and humour, fine descriptions of battle-fields and scenes; yet it is not history in the strict sense, it is merely personal biography, varied and enlivened by the author's rare genius and worship of power.

Although Carlyle had no remarkable analytic faculties, as a historical biographer he was really great. His insight of character and power of seizing reality, his power of discerning and selecting appropriate incidents and points, enabled him to shine and take the first rank in this branch of literature. Taking him all round, he was a real genius, a sagacious man, a noble and brave character.

Dr. W. F. Skene, Historiographer Royal for Scotland, has done much useful historical work. He edited the collection known under the title of " The Chronicles of the Picts and Scots," to which he prefixed an able introduction. He is the author of an admirable " History of Celtic Scotland," which was designed to ascertain and present what could be fairly extracted from the early authorities.

A transition from history to poetry is natural, as the two branches have many points of contact. Allan Ramsay's writings were pretty various, consisting of comic and satirical pieces, pastoral poems, songs, fables, and tales. His tales are humorous, but rather indelicate. Some of his songs are still favourites, such as " Lochaber no More," and " The Yellow Haired

Laddie." His greatest effort is "The Gentle Shepherd," which appeared in 1725, and was well received. He drew his shepherds and characters from real life, placed them in scenes which he had seen, and made them utter the idiomatic speech of their own native vales and hills. His skill is chiefly shown in the selection of his materials, in the grouping of his

THE HOUSE IN BROAD STREET, ABERDEEN, WHERE BYRON
LIVED WHEN A BOY.

natural and well-defined characters, and in the clear conception and elaboration of an interesting and romantic plot. Ramsay had many of the qualities of the real poet—imagination, the elaborative faculty, passion, humour, and pathos.

James Thomson, author of "The Seasons," "The

Castle of Indolence," and other poems, when a very young man proceeded to London to pursue his fortune, and after a hard struggle died in 1748, in the prime of life when he was working to his mental strength. His genius was luxuriant, glowing, and enthusiastic, and needed discipline. His feelings were warm and wide, embracing all mankind ; his love of nature was intense ; and his heart and soul throbbed with humanity.

THE COTTAGE WHERE BURNS WAS BORN.

Omitting many other poets of some note, I come to Robert Fergusson, a native of Edinburgh, who died in the twenty-third year of his age in 1774. His chief characteristics were a keen sense of the ludicrous, a strong vein of original comic humour, and a copious command of expressive language. Burns had an excessive admiration for the effusions of Fergusson and preferred them to Ramsay's. A few

lines from his piece, " Cauler Water," may indicate
why Burns admired him :—

> " When father Adie first pat spade in
>   The bonny yard o' ancient Edin,
>   His aumrie had nae liquor laid in
>   To fire his mou.
>   Nor did he thole his wife's upbraidin',
>   For bein' fou.
>
> .   .   .   .
>
>   His bairns had a' before the flood,
>   A langer tack o' flesh and blood,
>   And on mair pithy shanks they stood
>   Than Noah's line,
>   Wha still hae been a feckless brood,
>   Wi' drinkin' wine.
>   The fuddlin' bardies, nowadays,
>   Rin maukin wud in Bacchus' praise."

The first edition of Burns's poems was published
in 1786 ; and other three editions appeared in his
lifetime. Since his death ninety-three years ago,
upwards of three hundred editions of his poems have
been published. His influence on the imaginative
literature of Scotland has been deep and abiding.
The satirical and comic features of many of his
poems have had a most beneficial effect upon the
sentiments of the people ; as in conjunction with
other influences, they have enlightened their minds,
and enabled them to banish from their breasts a
host of delusive and absurd fears. Touching liberty
and independence, Burns's writings were clear and
emphatic. His own manly and independent spirit
shows itself in his poems and has had much effect

ROBERT BURNS.

on the nation. " The Tree of Liberty," and " A Man's a Man for a' that," were not written in vain.

Thomas Campbell's " Pleasures of Hope " appeared in 1799, when he was in his twenty-first year. The poem was immediately successful. It attracted many readers by its fine melody, polished style, and the generous sentiments which pervaded it. His short poems, and songs have been much admired, and some of the latter are popular favourites. His " Specimens of British Poets," with biographical and critical notices, published in 1818, is of much value; his criticisms are exceedingly just and interesting, and presented in a fine polished style.

Sir Walter Scott was a versatile genius, and attained distinction as a poet, a novelist, and in other branches of literature. From his childhood, he was a student of the ballad lore, the traditions, and superstitions of Scotland. His first independent poetic effort appeared in 1805, under the title of the " Lay of the Last Minstrel." It was very popular, and he was placed in the front rank of living poets. In 1808, his poem of " Marmion " was issued; and followed at short intervals by six or seven volumes of poetry. The " Lady of the Lake " was the most popular of his poems, and in a few months twenty thousand copies were sold. Though some of his poems are still read, they are not nearly so popular as his novels. Within a limited range of poetic conceptions which embraced an elaboration of past events and incidents, traditions and popular belief, Scott's poetry had merits of its own; but it lacked the glow of internal emotion, and that poetic fire generated in the mind and elaborated by intellectual energy.

SIR WALTER SCOTT.

James Hogg, a native of the vale of Ettrick, is best known by his poetic name of "The Ettrick Shepherd." He was sent to service when a boy, and received little education. But his mother had a habit of reciting legends and singing ballads, and many of her son's evenings in childhood were occupied in listening to her. He became an ardent reader of poetry and romances, and devoured the contents of a circulating library in Peebles. He assisted Sir Walter Scott in collecting ballads for the "Minstrelsy of the Border."

Hogg's first volume of songs and short pieces appeared in 1801. He acquired a facility of imitating the style of the old ballads ; and in 1807, he published " The Mountain Bard," a volume of songs and poems. His legendary poem entitled "The Queen's Wake" appeared in 1813. It consists of a number of tales and ballads supposed to be sung to Queen Mary of Scots by the native bards assembled at a royal wake in Holyrood, to show the fair Queen "the wondrous powers of Scottish song." The effort was well conceived and elaborated, and placed Hogg high in the rank of Scotch poets. At the end of it he adverted to an advice which Scott had once given him, to abstain from his worship of poetry :—

> " Even fairies sought our land again
> So powerful was his magic strain.
>   Blest be his generous heart for aye ;
>   He told me where the relic lay ;
>   Pointed my way with ready will
>   Afar on Ettrick's wildest hill ;
>   Watched my first notes with curious eye,
>   And wondered at my minstrelsy :

He little weened a parent's tongue
Such strains had o'er my cradle sung.
    But when to native feelings true,
I struck upon a chord was new ;
When by myself I 'gan to play,
He tried to wile my harp away.
Just when her notes began with skill,
To sound beneath the southern hill,
And twine around my bosom's core,
How could we part for evermore ?
'Twas kindness all—I cannot blame—
For bootless is the minstrel flame :
But sure a bard might well have known
Another's feelings by his own."

Hogg produced many works. "The Mador of the Moor," a poem in the Spenserian stanza ; "The Pilgrims of the Sun," in blank verse ; "Queen Hynde ;" "Dramatic Tales ;" several novels ; and "Jacobite Relics." He was an able and veritable genius. His imaginative and reproductive faculties were high, his sympathies wide, and his powers of realisation rarely excelled. There are passages in his writings which few poets have ever surpassed. The following lines are from his verses to the Comet of 1811 :—

" How lovely is this wildered scene,
    As twilight from her vaults so blue,
Steals soft o'er Yarrow's mountains green,
    To sleep embalmed in midnight dew ?
All hail, ye hills, whose towering height,
    Like shadows, scoops the yielding sky !
And thou, mysterious guest of night,
    Dread traveller of immensity.
Stranger of heaven ! I bid thee hail !
    Shred from the pall of glory riven,
That flashest in celestial gale,
    Broad pennon of the King of heaven,

Art thou the flag of woe and death,
　From angel's ensign staff unfurled?
Art thou the standard of His wrath
　Waved o'er a sordid, sinful world?

　　.　　　.　　　.　　　.　　　.　　　.

Whate'er protends thy front of fire,
　Thy streaming locks so lovely pale—
Or peace to man, or judgment dire,
　Stranger of heaven, I bid thee hail !

　　.　　　.　　　.　　　.　　　.　　　.

O on thy rapid prow to glide ;
　To sail the boundless skies with thee,
And plough the twinkling stars aside,
　Like foambells on a tranquil sea ;
To brush the embers from the sun,
　The icicles from off the pole ;
Then far to other systems run,
　Where other moons and planets roll."

It may be mentioned that the number of Scotch poets, whose names have been ascertained exceeds two thousand. In the Mitchell Library of Glasgow there are upwards of six thousand volumes of Scottish poetry and verse.

Turning to the region of fiction, some of Dr. Smollett's novels, which appeared in the middle of the last century, are still read. His " Roderick Random " was long a popular favourite. The taste and moral tone of Smollett's fiction is not of an elevated character ; but he had inventive power, native humour, and a wide range of knowledge. Between him and Scott there were a number of Scotch novelists, but the scale of this volume cannot admit of particularising them.

Sir Walter Scott was a man of wonderful and un-tiring industry. The quantity and variety of his

LOCH LOMOND.

22

works exceed that of any Scotch writer, although both in thought and style he has been frequently excelled in special branches of literature. In the field of the historic novel and romance of bygone centuries, drawn from the customs, the manners, the notions, and the superstitions of the Scottish people, Scott is unrivalled. His strength mainly lay in a facility of reproducing pictures and representations of the external action and superstition of past generations, and skill in weaving these into attractive and interesting stories. His novels have been exceedingly popular. Many millions of them have been sold. The moral tone of his fiction is manly and instructive ; but its original aim was to interest and amuse readers, and in this its success is unmatched.

John Galt was a contemporary of Scott, and the author of a long list of novels, tales, and various writings. He had great energy, but his genius was crippled by adverse circumstances. His life was one hard struggle, in which his brave spirit and warm heart never failed. In the perception of motive and character he was unsurpassed. But his taste was defective. The most popular of his novels were the " Wandering Jew," the " Ayrshire Legatees," and the " Annals of the Parish."

John Wilson, " Christopher North," was professor of moral philosophy in the University of Edinburgh from 1820 till his death in 1854, and was one of the leading contributors to *Blackwood's Magazine* in its palmy days. Some of his tales contain touching pictures and interesting scenes. He also wrote verse, but attained no distinction as a poet.

Miscellaneous literature would take in many names of note, but only a few can be mentioned. The religious literature of Scotland, in the form of sermons and hortative discourses, is large ; but in the department of theology there are few works of much authority, and till recently there was not the slightest necessity for them. For the religious differences among the Scots were not concerning the existence and attributes of God, or the fundamental doctrines of Christianity, but chiefly about forms of Church government and the powers of the Established Church, and the rights of congregations in relation to their ministers. Hence the characteristics of the religious literature of the nation.

Henry Home, Lord Kames, was called to the Scotch bar in 1732, and in 1752 was raised to the bench. He became a distinguished member of the literary circles of Edinburgh, a warm patron of literature, and of every movement calculated to promote the prosperity and civilisation of the nation. His writings were numerous, and treated of law, morality, religion, and other subjects. His " Elements of Criticism," if considered as.an attempt to investigate the principles of the fine arts as results of the operation of the mind, has merits, though it has many defects. The subject is difficult, and he was among the first to essay its explanation in modern times. His " Sketches of Man " contain some curious facts, pregnant hints, and acute reflections on society.

Thomas, Lord Erskine, the youngest son of the Earl of Buchan, served both in the army and navy, but resigned his commission, and turned to the study of law, and was called to the English bar in his twenty-eighth year. He soon attained a good position, and entered Parliament as member for Portsmouth in 1783. In 1806 he was appointed Lord Chancellor, but he had to retire on the dissolution of the Whig Government in the spring of 1807. He published in 1817 a political fragment, entitled, "Armata," which contains some good remarks on constitutional law and history.

Dr. Thomas Chalmers was the most distinguished of Scotch divines of the early part of this century. Prior to the Disruption he led the popular party in the General Assemblies of the Church. He was a popular preacher, delivered his sermons with intense earnestness, energy, and vehemence. He was appointed to the chair of divinity in the University of Edinburgh in 1828, but he relinquished it in 1843.

His collected works extend to thirty-four volumes, and treat of a wide range of subjects—theology, evidences of Christianity, moral philosophy, political economy, astronomical discourses, sermons, and other subjects. The chief characteristics of his writings were earnestness, energy, and profuse illustration. His knowledge was comprehensive and varied, both in literature and in science. He had also an unusually accurate appreciation of the feelings, the habits, and daily life of the people, which was the main source of his influence over the nation. In method and style his writings were defective. His usual mode of exposition was to present his main theme or idea in a variety of forms and from different points of view, with the aim of impressing it on the mind of his hearers.

Lord Jeffrey was called to the Scotch bar in 1794. He was one of the originators of *The Edinburgh Review*, which appeared in October, 1802, and from 1803 to 1829 was its editor and manager. In its pages he found ample scope for his political opinions, and his literary and critical faculties. The *Review* contributed much to raise the standard of criticism in Britain, and to advance more liberal principles in politics. Jeffrey collected the most important of his own contributions to the *Review*, and published them in 1844, in four volumes, since reprinted in one. His articles and criticisms embraced poetry, literature, and moral science. As a critic he showed sound judgment, good taste, and an elevated tone ; although occasionally in the early numbers of the *Review* he was harsh and severe. In poetic criticism he sometimes failed to appreciate the genuine merits of his author. I present a short specimen of his style on the prevailing notion that genius is a source of peculiar unhappiness to its possessor :—" Men of truly great powers of mind have generally been cheerful, social, and indulgent ; while a tendency to sentimental whining or fierce intolerance may be ranked among the surest symptoms of little souls and inferior intellects. In the whole list of our English poets we can only remember Shenstone and Savage—two, certainly of the lowest—who were querulous and discontented. Cowley, indeed, used to call himself melancholy ; but he was not in earnest, and, at any rate, was full of conceits and affectations, and has nothing to make us proud of him. Shakespeare, the greatest of them all, was evidently of a free and joyous temperament, and so was Chaucer their common master.   The same disposition appears to have predominated in Fletcher, Jonson, and their great contemporaries.   The genius of Milton partook something of the austerity of the party to which he belonged, and of the controversies in which he was

HOUSE OF JAMIESON, THE SCOTCH VANDYCK, AT ABERDEEN.
(*Lately demolished.*)

involved ; but even when fallen on evil days and evil tongues, his spirit seems to have retained its serenity, as well as its dignity ; and in his private life, as well as in his poetry, the majesty of a high character is tempered with great sweetness, genial indulgences, and practical wisdom.   In the succeeding age our poets were but too gay ; and though we forbear to speak of living authors, we know enough of them to say with confidence, that to be miserable or to be hated is not now, any more than heretofore, the common lot of those who excel."

Dr. John Tulloch was the author of a number of works, chiefly theological and historical. His first notable effort was a treatise on Theism which received one of the Burnett prizes in 1855. His most elaborate work is " Rational Theology and Christian Philosophy of England in the Seventeenth Century." Its method is historic and expositive, and it is full of instruction and interest. Dr. Tulloch contemplated writing the modern history of Scotland, and had made some progress in preparing materials in 1877 ; but unhappily he did not live to finish it. For several years he edited *Fraser's Magazine*, and contributed to its pages various critical and literary articles. His style is clear, easy, polished, and flowing, but rather lacking in strength. In describing individual men and their opinions his expression is often exceedingly fine and happy.

In conclusion, this story has necessarily been brief. But the origin and the long and chequered career of the nation have been indicated in a connected form. It may fitly be added, that during the past hundred and fifty years the nation has made vast progress in almost every department of industry, science, and art. Many entirely new industries have been created and developed. Medical schools have been instituted and organised, which have attained a high and wide reputation. A school of mental philosophy was founded by Francis Hutcheson in the second quarter of the last century, which embraces in its roll the names of Hume, Adam Smith, Reid, Stewart, Campbell, Brown, Mackintosh, Hamilton, Ferrier, Bain, and many others. The efforts of the Scotch school were mainly concentrated on psychology—the explanation of the human mind, and moral and political science. The works which have emanated from it contain a body of doctrines and reflections which are well worth careful study and examination. For, after all, the mind alone constitutes the glory and the dignity of man. In the circle of fine art there has been a marked advance. The progress of painting and sculpture has been a striking feature in the recent history of the nation. Schools of art and art galleries have sprung into existence in all the chief centres of population in the kingdom. Let us hope that the culture of art shall be still more widely diffused, and the avenues of elevated feeling and refined enjoyment expanded.

ELLEN'S ISLE, LOCH KATRINE.

INDEX.